PRAISE FOR THE REVOLUTION WE EXPECTED

"In *The Revolution We Expected*, Naranjo syntheses his lifelong study of ancient philosophy and humanistic psychology, then offers a hopeful path forward, beyond a society ruled by dogma, greed, authoritarianism, and narcissism. He envisions a future that begins with generosity, self-awareness, and a culture that nourishes those qualities in our children.
— Don Lattin, author, *Changing Our Minds,*
The Harvard Psychedelic Club

"Claudio Naranjo is recognized as one of the most creative and experienced explorers of human potential extant. He was also a psychotherapist, medical doctor, author, educator, Buddhist practitioner, and pioneer in the area of psychedelic therapies. His integrative approaches to a multiplicity of fields elevates his work and creates global reach and influence. In *The Revolution We Expected,* Naranjo points strongly to the need for emotional education—an education for wisdom and not merely knowledge to be harnessed for financial gain. This book is indeed a gift to this and future generations as we navigate the turbulent waters ahead."
— Allan Badiner, author, activist, co-editor
Zig Zag Zen: Buddhism and Psychedelics

"Claudio Naranjo was a brilliantly creative pioneer of the human potential. Along with his passion for personal transformation, he was also deeply committed to social transformation. This manifested in a truly integral approach to education and human development. Drawing on vast intellectual resources and on the great depth of his personal experience, this volume is a remarkable synthesis of his life's work."

— Alfonso Montuori Ph.D., professor
California Institute of Integral Studies

The Revolution We Expected

THE
Revolution
We Expected

Cultivating a
New Politics of
Consciousness

CLAUDIO NARANJO

SYNERGETICPRESS
regenerating people and planet

SANTA FE & LONDON

Published by Synergetic Press 1 Bluebird Court, Santa Fe, NM 87508 & 24 Old Gloucester St. London, WC1N 3AL England

LIBRARY OF CONGRESS CATALOGING-IN-PUBLICATION DATA

Names: Naranjo, Claudio, author.
Title: The revolution we expected : cultivating a new politics of
    consciousness / Claudio Naranjo.
Description: Santa Fe, NM : Synergetic Press, [2020]
Identifiers: LCCN 2020027985 (print) | LCCN 2020027986 (ebook) | ISBN
    9780907791829 (paperback) | ISBN 9780907791805 (ebook)
Subjects: LCSH: Social change. | Enneagram.
Classification: LCC HM831 .N36 2020 (print) | LCC HM831 (ebook) |
DDC
    303.4--dc23
LC record available at https://lccn.loc.gov/2020027985
LC ebook record available at https://lccn.loc.gov/2020027986

Translated by Lawrence Schimel
Cover and book design by Ann Lowe
Cover photo by Raquel Diaz
Managing Editor: Amanda Müller
Printed by Versa Press, USA on 55# Tradebook Cream
Typeface: Agency and Garamond

TABLE OF CONTENTS

PROLOGUE

WE ARE IN THE MIDST OF A REVOLUTION, yet we do not recognize it as the one we were waiting for. In the first place, we had already stopped hoping for it, but moreover we had imagined it as one we would create ourselves, whereas this one seems to be happening on its own. Nonetheless, I think that when the transformation that has already begun has taken place, we will say that it is the one we had always hoped for, just that we had not known how to envisage it correctly.

On the one hand, until now we have only known political and ideological revolutions, and what is taking place now is a revolution of awareness. On the other hand, we have never had less belief in our ability to change anything in the world in which we live, and we have even lost the zeal for utopian thinking that existed in times past. It is rightly said that utopias help us advance and the very rejection of this utopian thinking is paralyzing.

The Chilean sociologist Antonio Elizalde has compared the disappearance of utopian thinking with the process that takes place while training fleas, something that is well-known among flea trainers but almost unheard of for the rest of us: the flea is placed in a transparent flask with a similarly transparent top and one simply waits for the flea to learn, after systematically banging its head against the invisible walls of the container with its more energetic leaps, to take smaller leaps and thereby suffer less.

The metaphor proves particularly apt if we superimpose it on that of the domestication of elephants, as Elizalde does. The elephant tied to a tree by its leg learns that it must let go of the suffering of its fruitless and painful efforts; this learning prevails in its behavior even when it has grown to such a degree that it could easily uproot the tree.

The fact is that today, we do not even take great leaps when it comes to thinking, at a time when the eminent theories are mistrusted as if they had only served to trick us, with the result that not only does impotence spread but also justifications for it. It is my hope that we are mobilized by seeing how our situation resembles that of a frog in a pot being heated slowly, something that doesn't trouble it because its skin only has receptors that detect abrupt changes in temperature.

I have titled my first chapter "For a Politics of Consciousness," because I think that the primary problem in the world, beyond its many symptoms, is unawareness and that only in waking from our blind somnambulism can we evolve.

I continue, after some passing reflections, toward what could be a possible education—since, if we want increased consciousness, we must start with education—as nothing can offer us as much as the transformation of education in order to transform our civilization during this crisis of obsolescence. Much of what has been written about my vision of an education that is more relevant to human development was formulated before being asked to write this book. It was a result of being invited to open the seventh World Conference on Higher Education, in 2010, with the title "Educating for Sustainability," and since then I have wanted to include a brief preface to the chapters, in which I outline the subjects of what could come to be an education for freedom, love, and wisdom.

The understanding of the limitations of a merely utilitarian environment (which made use of rational arguments and mathematical statistical data when inducing people to do things like taking care of non-renewable resources) has led to the formulation of 'deep ecology', which includes consideration of the emotional and ethical dimension of things. I think that likewise, the results of an education that tried to tackle the urgent issue of sustainability through merely rational teaching, such as the education which prevails in today's world—and still makes its presence felt in the incipient attempts at emotional education—would be limited without coming to truly touch our emotions or our moral life.

After a series of chapters that dwell on education (beginning with the subject of emancipatory education, which despite being indispensable is always relegated, followed by subjects necessary for the development of love and then with the subject of an education for wisdom), which is prolonged in a chapter dedicated to the potential of meditation in the educational realm, I devote a chapter to my own contribution to the training of educators. These are the Seekers After Truth (SAT) Programs, a curriculum for the development of the three loves and the three fundamental aspects of attention: living in the here and now, psychological self-awareness, and deeper spiritual self-awareness.

I then devote a chapter to what could be a transformation of the business world, a trampoline that is perhaps necessary for a transformation of the economy, and I conclude with the idea of the awakening of global consciousness as the most decisive issue in the revolution we are experiencing, given the close relationship of the consciousness of the community with the power that legitimizes or delegitimizes the remaining powers.

I began to compile this book at the invitation of the Italian magazine *Terra Nova* and presently I have yet to contact its editor to find out if they are still interested in publishing it. Whatever the case may be, I am glad to have written it, because it sounds to me rather like a sociopolitical testament and I am inclined to believe that it will have a fruitful impact.

I lay out many things in the following pages that I have already said in earlier books but conceived for a different audience; since when I was younger, I spoke more to the old guard and the authorities but now that I am in my eighties, it seems to me that it makes more sense for me to address primarily the youth: those on whom it will fall to be the founders of a post-patriarchal society and for me to try to speak with the greatest possible simplicity, leaving aside my old academic habits.

A North American Sufi (E.J. Gold) once explained, in answer to a seeker's question as to whether the work of the liberation of the ego should always be considered war, that the matter could be understood by considering the story of a man who sought an alternative to the amputation that all the surgeons recommended to treat a malignant tumor in his penis. Having placed his hopes in the arts of a Chinese medic who had performed apparent miracles using nothing more than acupuncture and herbs, he went to the place where this medic practiced and finally volunteered to undergo a careful examination. As the wise, traditional medic slowly examined his pulse, a slight smile grew on his lips, so the patient excitedly asked him, "You don't need to cut?"

"No!" responded the wise man immediately, quickly adding, "It will fall off by itself."

Since hearing this application of the joke to spiritual work, I have often repeated it myself, to thereby transmit a conviction that when self-awareness is sufficiently deep, our problematic quirks of character lose power and end up transforming into abilities that serve our best intentions. However, until recently I had never laid hands on this anecdote as an explanation of the sociopolitical problem of our world in crisis. This is because it is a novelty for us to be witnessing the beginning of a spontaneous crumbling of that patriarchal power to which we can attribute practically all the evils of the civilized world.

Just as certain biological species seem to have become extinct because of their failure to adapt, our consumerist society has reached the limits of its sustainability, such that we now witness not just the collapse of our economy but also

the beginning of a massive delegitimization of our governments and their implicit ideologies. All this, which Marxism
highlighted as being the enemy of humanity, seems to be
starting to sink now, just like a ship that is letting in water,
which cannot be saved either by the words of its on-board
officers or by successive repairs.

Even if the catastrophe of the sinking of the patriarchal
vessel in which we have been sailing continues, it is better for
us to understand, by our going through our crisis with faith,
that the agonizing death rattles of our civilization are our
greatest hope of regeneration.

During the last ten years of my life, I have again become
an activist with the determination to change education in
order to change the world (as the title of one of my books
suggests) and over this time I have been surprised by the
contrast between my good reasons and my scant success in
taking my work about awareness to educational institutions.
Recently, I have come to think that my activism was headed
in an erroneous direction and that more could be expected
from the help we offer outside rather than within the system,
with its fossilized bureaucracies and its governmental direc-
tives, which until now have always fostered the status quo.
I have even come to question the scope of the apparently

successful work I have been doing, which despite profoundly influencing the lives of many people in many countries year after year, would be unlikely to ever transform our dying institutions. I am nonetheless consoled by thinking that the work of witnessing people's psycho spiritual maturation will be an inheritance for those who—engaged in the rescue operation during our great shipwreck—will have the opportunity of constructing a new world.

Once again in the history of our species, we find ourselves facing something resembling the mythical great flood, which our ancestors interpreted as an act by which God punished a corrupt world with annihilation and prepared a new start; only we no longer think of God as an indignant father but rather as a cosmic organism fueled by implacable laws, wiser than those which have fueled our ill-considered legislation, our predatory economy, and our poor culture in which the values of life have come to be subordinate to those of the stock exchange, as well as to the counter values of an egocentric and narcissistic patriarchal ego.

Ever since the Sumerians invented writing five thousand years ago, allegorical stories about a great transformation which some human beings underwent via some kind of inner journey have been passed on; a transformation that moves from a death of their ordinary and larval form of existence to the gestation of a new, semi-divine life. This metamorphosis, which is possible for the human being and is the subject of numerous legends of heroes, has only been directly experienced by a few over the course of our long history, but it seems that in our time many feel called to the great adventure of awareness, as if we have to take a step in our collective evolution comparable to that told by the book of Exodus, in which an entire people crossed the Red Sea to emerge from slavery in pursuit of the Promised Land.

Furthermore, it would seem that in our era, for the first time, a process is being outlined during this twilight of the hegemonic Western civilization in which the presence of the nascent manifestations of a new world is felt, a world freed from the millennium of patriarchal power: a death/rebirth on a collective scale, beyond any of the various extinctions of past civilizations or the emerging of new ones.

What should be done, then, in these times in which the worsening ineffectiveness of the politico-economic system that we have created is leading to catastrophic levels of poverty, hunger, unhealthiness, and environmental, ethical, and cultural degradation?

As opposed to times past, during which a revolutionary attitude meant opposing the enemies of the common good, today, when as in the anecdote of the Chinese medic, evil "will fall away by itself," it would seem that the priority would be for the community to take charge of what traditional institutions have neglected and will surely further neglect at the moment of their collapse; something that has already been happening for decades now through those innumerable civil organizations that the UN has called non-governmental.

There are many necessary tasks and Edgar Morin has lucidly set out a number of them in his recent book, *La Voie*. There are also a large number of people who, being unemployed, can offer a hand. It is even conceivable that the agricultural excesses could feed them, if the community prevailed over the commercial desire to destroy them in order to protect their market value.

However, even the most complete treatment of the symptoms of an illness will fail if not enough attention is paid to its root. I hope that the emphasis that I have given in my vision of the patriarchal ego, as well as the corresponding emphasis that I propose that we give to the formulation of an education in order to emerge from the patriarchy in my proposed corrective action, justify the publication of this book, whose contents could perhaps be an inspiration for those to whom the building of a future world falls.

CHAPTER 1
For a Politics of Consciousness

I N TITLING THIS CHAPTER "For a Politics of Consciousness," my intention is to imply that what we have now is a politics of unconsciousness, which is something that goes beyond the simple proposition that unconsciousness rules in the world.

Certainly, there was a time when most people suffered the consequences of that limitation that we associate with the Freudian unconscious: they repressed certain ugly things, by not admitting that we are aggressive, selfish, and in many ways like animals. During what is called the Victorian era, people lived an enormous lie regarding their goodness and there were numerous subjects that were not talked about, nor publicly recognized. Nevertheless, it seems to me that much of this has changed through culture and art.

Today, the things that are taboo subjects for discussion are not our sexual or aggressive desires. Instead, one could now say that we have a political unconscious. It is as if world politics needed us to be unaware individuals and to exercise certain influences in order to keep us barely able to think for ourselves.

I do not propose to speak only of unconsciousness and of how much it would help us to become more aware, but instead, more broadly, I intend to speak of evil: of the roots of evil and of what we could do to improve the world in these critical times if we were to pay attention to what we know about evil and discontent.

In speaking of the 'roots of evil' I simply want to review what we know on a relatively rational and scientific level about our destructiveness. Even before the birth of that science, there were people in the world who thought clearly but it was with the advent of psychology that illness in a sense that goes beyond the physical began to be discussed. To speak of illness on a psychological level is to talk as much about evil as of discontent; or, in other words, destructiveness and suffering.

It was earlier believed that we were destructive by nature, such that human nature would be more wolf-like than that of wolves themselves, and the notion that we are intrinsically destructive was shared by Freud and Melanie Klein. None-theless it seems to me that the progress of therapeutic culture has shown that people can improve, even if not completely, to a certain degree. The fact that some people are feeling better and acting better, becoming more loving and less destructive as the echoes of childhood suffering diminish, makes outdated this idea that evil is intrinsic, particularly in the realm of humanist psychology.

There used to be much talk of *the fall of man* (of man and not of woman, although it was thought that woman was the cause of the fall of man) and even more blame was cast upon the serpent, who had, in the times before the famous book of Genesis, symbolized the Mother Goddess and the forces of Nature; that is to say, the natural world. People talked of "The Fall" and of sin before they talked of illness and the inappropriateness of the word "sin" in our time is that the connotation of the term has changed. The ancients understood sin to be a deviation of psychic energy, tied to an error of perspective. Centuries of punitive ecclesiastical authoritarianism gave the term not just an additional condemnatory meaning but also a normative and moralist point of reference, that makes it less useful than the broad modern notion of emotional disturbance, which in turn suggests a relationship with a state of incomplete development or of psychological immaturity.

When Medieval Christianity spoke of sins, the idea of error was very present, as well as that of deviation and it seems to me that when someone who has come to fully understand some of those old sins they do not just feel that they have acted badly (in the face of what they are shown to be guilty or ashamed of) but they also come to understand that they have been wrong. It is a great thing when someone understands that they have followed a wrong path in life. That they have been living for appearances for example; or for money and not for what they truly want to do; or that they have been living as a slave to external pressures, without following their own heart. There are those who at a given moment come to say: "No!" Christianity has called that moment the *metanoia*, or sometimes the conversion; although the word "conversion" has also come to be understood as the adoption of a certain creed, which entails a more superficial act than "change of mind" or *metanoia*, which is the expression of a transformation; a kind of metamorphosis that is part of human destiny.

We are beings that have a larval state and a mature state, which are considerably different. But not much is known about this. It does not form part of our culture to inform ourselves about this matter, because we are in a culture in which there are almost no mature beings. We are in a culture that has been kept immature through a sort of emotional plague, as Wilhelm Reich said; an emotional plague that is perpetuated over the generations, interfering in the emotional growth that could lead people to fully express their potential.

My theme might very well be stated as: "What would we need to do if we kept in mind the theories of neurosis?" Save that "theory of neurosis" is too modern a term and at the same time somewhat outdated, given that, unfortunately, the word "neurosis" is disappearing from the lexicon of psychopathology. It was a very useful word because it alluded to a unity behind many syndromes of many apparently diverse manifestations of emotional pathology. Now (at least in North American academic psychology, embodied in the DSM-V), only the surface of different syndromes is recognized, without the idea of their common root. The idea of neurosis was very convenient.

Nonetheless, I will take the liberty of talking about "theories of neurosis" from before scientific psychology. Are they perhaps less true than the psychoanalytical vision that Buddha offered regarding the roots of suffering?

The theory of neurosis formulated by Buddha as an interpretation of the Samsara, which is the name given in

Buddhism to the ordinary condition of the mind and which literally means "to go around in circles," is great. Buddha said that suffering and evil stemmed from our being ignorant.

While this theory could at first glance seem somewhat antiquated and simplistic to a person of our present time, that is because we modern people have already forgotten what it is to be ignorant and we think that ignorance consists of someone lacking some piece of information. The educators of today seem interested only in information, whereas the ancients were more interested in wisdom and they understood this to be the ability to see things as they are.

Seeing things as they are does not depend just on information or even on reason, given that it requires us to have an ability to see things as a whole, and also to grasp them in their context. This Gestalt ability of perception, we know today, is an integrative ability of our right cerebral hemisphere and cannot be replaced by the discursive thinking that comes through the analysis of the separate elements. Our analytical brain that embodies our hunter's mind and is focused on grabbing and acquiring things, culminates in our scientific and technological capability, that has inspired the myth of progress of the modern world. Undoubtedly there has been immense scientific and technological progress in our recent history, but it has been a problematic progress insomuch as while we progressed in this regard, something has been lost, corrupted, or complicated. The right hemisphere, that is usually the wise brain and perceives things in their entirety, allows for metaphorical thinking and sustains our values and our capacity for empathy, has become practically inaccessible, because our left brain (which we can characterize as our shrewd brain) tends to lose itself in its own conversations with itself, becoming functionally insular. We enclose ourselves in our thoughts and we become dogmatic in turning our science into arrogance: the negation of all intuitive knowledge, beginning with our perception of the obvious.

There was a period when educators thought that humanism was necessary, that it was important to read the classics (especially the Greeks and Latins) who began to be discovered after the monopoly of Christianity during the Middle Ages. It was thought that there would be a transmission of certain capacities (the civic virtues of the Romans, for example), attitudes that cannot be explained very easily but which are passed on through art and literature.

Unfortunately, however, humanism has transformed into yet another encyclopedia, so that it is read with philological or academic interest, or it is read to find out things that can later be flaunted as signs of culture in a time in which culture is no longer the cultivation of the mind but instead a coat of varnish, just for show. Humanism has not fulfilled that original purpose of passing on humanity, and even the arts are disappearing from school curricula today, since those who make decisions about educational policies prefer to prepare people for the strategic thinking that is required in production and in commercial business. Not even parents defend their children's right to be educated in order to be more human and now that it is so clear that getting good grades in school enables people to find a job, parents to a certain degree succumb to the temptation of having their children sell their souls to the devil, concerning themselves above all with their future work prospects. They therefore learn to pass exams and they learn under pressure, although not with a view to the extrinsic recompense of learning nor the fact that passing exams favors maturation. Neither does it favor true knowledge, nor the true understanding of things, which would mark the beginning of wisdom.

It is said of wisdom that it is an understanding of things that requires something more than our discursive and instrumental analytical thinking, which is the specialized function of one of our brains that in our recent history has come to eclipse our intuitive hemisphere. Ian McGilchrist, in his recent work on the relationship between the cerebral hemispheres, suggests that just as we have two eyes which see from two different angles, thereby giving us the ability to see in depth, we have two brains that offer us complementary ways of seeing, since they process information in different ways so that we can establish a synthesis between the voice of wisdom and that of practical reason. He proposes that the voice of our right hemisphere is that of our inner master, while the voice of our left, verbal hemisphere is that of a less profound intelligence that has usurped the master's mantle.[1]

If we wish to recover that wisdom that not just Buddha but also Socrates and Saint Augustine considered to be the antidote to that ignorance that is the source of our suffering and our destructiveness, we must recover our intuitive thinking, which is the faculty that operates in the time-honored sages' comprehension of complex thinking. It is worth remembering that what science knows at one specific moment in history is worth little a few years later but we still read Shakespeare, who lived some 500 years ago and Homer, who lived more than two thousand years ago and even the epic of Gilgamesh, who was born in Sumer during the time when writing was invented. Humanism appeals to something more invariable

[1] Iain McGilchrist: *The Master and His Emissary.* Yale University Press. New Haven, 2009.

than science and despite the scientific prejudice that has obfuscated the legacy of the Age of Enlightenment, wisdom is somewhat more profound than shrewdness.

We can continue to think, then, that Buddha and Socrates are still right and that an important root of suffering and destructiveness in human life is a sort of blindness that does not see things as they are and that this blindness is perfectly compatible with analytical knowledge, literacy and an abundance of information. Today we live in a world that is very well informed and that knows many things, but it is an educated ignorance that does not see obvious things, or at least does not act wisely.

Let us take for example economic science. Everyone knows that the owners of the world in practice are no longer the governors and even less so the people but rather the economists. At least, it could be said that the governors invoke the authority of the economists, so that the economy is an instrument of politics. However, to a growing degree, the economists are the ones who make the important decisions, along with the bankers, as if there were no doubt that they are the most qualified guides for humanity. The problem is that the more power we give the economists, the more economic problems we have. The entire world realizes this. There are already people who are starting to review the economy and one of the criticisms that is beginning to be made now, after the economic crisis of 2008, is that the economists did not know how to predict this crisis that they themselves caused with an economic science that in reality is not so scientific but is instead a justification of customary economic practices. Some economists began to say that the system of commercial equations that make up the body of the economy does not take into account human or environmental considerations. Can one consider as scientific a vision that conceives of such an arbitrary, closed system when the reality is an open system, considers the buying and selling of work and goods as if they existed in a world separate from humans and nature, ignoring such obvious things as the impossibility of an indefinite industrial growth in a finite environment?

Even the most scientific things then, are sometimes biased by a lack of vision. I very much enjoy the work by José Saramago titled *Blindness*, which is a great metaphor of how much damage is done when people cannot see. It seems that collectively, there are things that are not seen and the fact that one can logically justify what is done in this blindness, covers up and perpetuates the ignorance. In other words, what is seen very clearly with the shrewd brain, covers up our stupidity.

It seems that we have lost the use of our wise and creative brain, which is like the master brain within ourselves and which our technocratic, barbarian shrewdness has usurped.

McGilchrist, in his aforementioned book, notes that Nietzsche recounts in one of his works the story of a wise master who was a king and, in his territory, there lived very happy subjects, since prosperity reigned in virtue of his wisdom. However, when the kingdom began to expand, this king needed to name delegates or emissaries to govern the provinces and they took charge of the details, because he could no longer be in all places nor move about so much. He trusted his emissaries, and what is more: he *needed* to trust them in order for the kingdom to function. However one of his emissaries, who knew the details of the things that were happening, thought that the master did not know as much as he did and considering himself to be better informed, he ended up usurping the master and using the master's mantle to give himself authority.

McGilchrist says that we all carry within us a wise brain (the master, that is to say, the one who should rule) but his emissary, (the shrewd brain, which takes care of the details, such as accounting (the brain of the *homo economicus*) has already usurped that power and the master is nowhere to be seen, since our culture has locked him away, forgetting about him.

What would be worthwhile for us to do if we took into consideration that ancient but almost obvious theory (which was not just that of Buddha and Socrates but also Saint Augustine) according to which the primary root of evil and suffering is ignorance, which prevents us from seeing things as they are?

Obviously, we would have to concern ourselves a lot with what we call wisdom but about which we have only a very vague notion, since we have forgotten what it is about. We barely understand that it is not the same as knowledge, but we do not know the difference between intellectual knowledge and that other level of knowing that we recognize as the knowledge of the wise. We could say the knowledge of the "visionaries," as they are usually called today, although we feel that it is a case of something not just uncommon but also questionable. Above all, this has been the case since what happened in the Age of Enlightenment, in which, to undo the Church's authoritarianism, the European World turned against that which is called faith, which was confused with the credo of the Catholic church, despite the fact that this was, in reality, dogma rather than faith. Faith, in truth, is intuition, that is to say a different knowledge from rational knowledge, a way of understanding that which today, from a scientific point of view, we feel is invalid.

This would be the first corollary of the diagnosis that ignorance is at the root of our ills and in the search for wisdom surely, we would be interested by the idea that, by not understanding our Being, we distract ourselves too much with appearances. Nevertheless, once we establish in our agendas the search for that mysterious wisdom, we must ask ourselves how we can become wiser.

Obviously, this can be done through culture, through education, primarily; and perhaps through the institutions that care for our health, because wisdom is something that makes us complete and without which we are like cripples, so it concerns mental health. But how?

Given what we know about the working of our cerebral hemispheres we can understand how on target the approaches of yoga and the practices of meditation or contemplation have been, which lead to mental silence and stillness; since if it is true that we do not manage to *listen* to our *wise* cerebral hemisphere because of the exclusive attention we give to our shrewd hunter or advantage-seeking brain, one can understand that nothing would be more pertinent to that contact we are lacking in our more holistic perceptions and without our sense of values, than silencing that noise of thought that isolates us from our experiential contact with the present moment. Anyone who tries this will also understand that in order to silence our thinking one must also silence that compulsion to go in search of the next moment and its potential satisfaction, which seems to comprise the omni-present motivation of that thinking; in other words, to reach that which the Chinese call *wu wei*; or non-action, that is only possible when one achieves spiritual peace.

Let us now consider a second notion about the causes of suffering. Why has our consciousness degraded? Practically at the same time that the notion of ignorance as the root of suffering was formulated in India, the idea appeared that we suffer (and cause suffering) because of something that could be called *hyperdesire*. When translating Buddhist or Hindu texts, they frequently talk only of desire, but it would be more correct in these cases to refer to extreme desire or attachment and the psychoanalytic term *orality* is especially relevant, referring to what a child who has suffered frustration in its maternal care develops. In response to this childhood frustration, the child remains conditioned by an excessive insistence, as if this could compensate the lack the child experienced and that explicit insistence or hyperdesire converts the child into a *leech*. There are many leeches in the world and no matter how much this affective dependence is associated to an implicit idea that the lure or nostalgia lead to satisfaction, the opposite is true.

Kierkegaard was right in saying that the door to paradise was opened from within; for the harder one pushes, the more difficult it is to gain access. A leech-like or excessively needy attitude toward life is disadvantageous or dysfunctional, since it is the opposite of receptivity. It is when one is receptive that one receives and not when one pushes, insists, or protests, attitudes that are comparable in their scant results to the behavior of a child who in his excessive greed bites the nipple of the mother who nurses him.

Schopenhauer took this idea of suffering due to our excessive desires from oriental philosophy and as a result proposed that in order to be happier, we must reduce our desires; as had already been proposed by Epicurus, the somewhat marginal contemporary of Aristotle. Epicurus was criticized quite a lot in his day, in the first place because anyone who wanted to teach philosophy as a contemporary of Aristotle, who dominated the field, was rebuked but also because he was interested in a subject that was unacceptable to philosophers: happiness. What an irrelevant subject happiness had seemed to the philosophers. In the entire history of philosophy, little had been said about happiness. In addition, Epicurus was very interested in friendship, community living, and women in his community. It was also said that he held orgies, although it seems that this was more a product of the fantasy of his enemies. Epicurus' primary message is that in order to be happy one must be content with less, since a large part of unhappiness arises from the frustration of excessive desires. Nonetheless, he went further than Schopenhauer in his proposal, because he suggested that in order to not have excessive desires it was important to cultivate neutrality, a suggestion that Buddha also taught: something like how to let the mind go deeper inward, where it starts to feel at home, in a warm quiescence that nurtures it, making it independent of the customary satisfactions in the external world.

These are difficult things to explain for people who work only with concepts derived from the external world. Pascal though, was able to describe something similar, because he said that most of the world's problems derived from people not knowing how to remain still in their own rooms, instead they go about everywhere wanting to stick their noses into the lives of others.

The question about the antidote to greed leads us again then, to what has already been said about the antidote to that ignorance that is the result of a disconnection from our inspired wisdom. Most people have not even realized their inability to be still, which is a result of the impossibility of their own minds resting in the present moment. We do not even notice this lack of inner peace and we are in a world that stimulates us with increasing urgency to run hurriedly toward the future. As if on a carousel, we look for the next thing or the next thought with an eagerness nourished by an implicit dissatisfaction and a belief that the next moment, or the next fulfilled desire, will bring us what we are searching for.

Both in the spiritual culture in India as well as in Greece, the value of mitigating our excessive desires with the cultivation of an imperturbable neutrality that lies in the depths of our minds were very much borne in mind. The Greeks personified this power of neutrality in the figure of a god, Apollo, who did not just symbolize this knowledge itself (which places the soul in harmony) but also the neutral distance that makes possible the clarity of self-awareness.

Fritz Perls, the originator of Gestalt therapy (which psychoanalysis evolved into in the 1960s), popularized the expression *here and now*, which is repeated with constantly greater appreciation to the degree that one discovers the existential treasure contained within it. The power of the here and now does not only lie in the fact of us becoming aware that our mental processes introduce an element of corrective feedback into our experience but also that the very ability to be present has an optimizing effect on our life. Why? Because we are potentially conscious beings and consciousness is pure, no matter how much our daily lives have become comparable to a sleepwalking existence. That is to say: we have consciousness and we have desires; we have consciousness and we have impulses, aversions, instinctive impulses, diverse emotions and we have of course an awareness of our thoughts and not just of our feelings and perceptions. In summary, we have mental phenomena, but it is as if consciousness were not another mental phenomenon rather the root of all mental phenomena, or a fundamental state beyond that of thinking, feeling and wanting. Thoughts come and go, emotions are short-lived, as Buddhism insists with such emphasis. Everything that happens is ephemeral but although we are always faced with the spectacle of a fleeting world, like dreams or the shapes of the clouds, our very consciousness is something that can be compared to space, which is just a field that contains everything and lacks its own characteristics.

The greatest wise men of all time, in all cultures, have known that condition of recognizing consciousness itself: a condition in which one understands like an impartial witness of oneself and which some people occasionally arrive at through life experience and its frustrations. Although sometimes it is the pain of misfortune that leads to the wisdom of detachment, it can also be cultivated with spiritual practice. The result is transformed into something resembling a distance from things but that is not a forced distance, rather it is a condition comparable to that of a child who no longer needs his old toys and leaves them behind. The same satisfaction obtained from our juvenile passions can contribute to us eventually distancing ourselves from them as we get older, in the best sense of the word, freeing ourselves from so many desires and simplifying our lives.

It is said that at the entrance to the Temple of Apollo there was an inscription that read: "Nothing in excess," and Greek culture gave great importance to this moderation of appetites; not in a puritan form—as came to happen later with Christianity—and not so much to do with sex but rather in terms of food. Moderation in eating revealed which people were noble, the ideal of nobility being a person with self-control and one who did not have so many needs. That revealed an ideal of being more independent of the body and its needs, which was part of the Apollonian spirit. Far from dismissing that ideal as a whim of Greek culture, we also need today that neutral consciousness known to those who have undertaken a therapeutic or spiritual path and have managed to recognize their exaggerated, neurotic needs for applause, affection, support or confirmation, mothering or guidance. All these needs belong to infancy and diminish with maturity, especially through self-awareness and becoming more conscious of oneself.

If we wish to intervene collectively to achieve a better world, then, self-awareness is very important. Socrates said that an unexamined life is not worth living, but what does education do to show us how to be more aware? On the contrary: it busies our minds excessively with absorbing information and maintaining arbitrary disciplines. It is not just lamentable but also laughable, that after the passing of the greatest educator in the world, the philosopher who showed us the path of self-awareness, contemporary education is not taking it seriously. Education is so enormously interested in the external world that it almost looks suspiciously at the proposal of a "path of self-awareness." The self-awareness lacuna is not filled by teaching psychology or philosophy, since self-awareness is a guided process of awareness in which one person has to lead the other by the hand, similar to how the playing of a musical instrument is taught.

Let us now consider a third theory of neurosis: according to which we suffer because of certain interior states that are comparable to parasites of the mind, which take possession of our energies. In the Christian world, the cardinal sins were the dominant vision of evil and discontent in the Middle Ages and today, it could seem to us that those "sins" are a dogmatic residue of the past, of little or doubtful relevance to our lives. Nonetheless, Eastern culture had something similar in the *kleshas* of the Hindu tradition, emotional obstacles, which are more or less the same: pride, for example, or envy. Why those states and not others? Among so many negative emotions, why did the Christian tradition choose the seven cardinal sins, or Buddhism the customary five? In Christianity before Gregory the Great, the Pope who systematized the seven sins, there were eight of them and in recent times a system of nine is becoming known based around what is called the Enneagram, the nine-point figure that is said to be emblematic of an Asian tradition of Christianity that has reached us from Afghanistan and which was first mentioned by George Gurdjieff. Whether there are seven, eight, or nine sins and no matter how inconvenient it seems to us, is it justifiable to call them 'cardinal sins', intimating that in their totality they make up the roots of our many apparent ills?

As a first attempt at a response, we can see that psychology has been rediscovering these same mental states. Thus, for example, a few decades ago Karen Horney built an entire theoretical and psychotherapeutic system around pride and specifically around the idea that we are losing our lives by living for glory more than for the realization of all our potential. To live for glory is to live from the perspective of an idealized self, in such a way that we think we are realizing ourselves when we are only realizing an idealized image that we have constructed of ourselves. We construct this idealized image based on a contemptuous vision of ourselves that has formed in our minds because we were not loved enough, or because as a consequence we did not learn to love ourselves, to value ourselves. Melanie Klein did something similar with envy and Freud as well when proposing fear and anxiety as the base of all our neurotic problems. From practically each one of the cardinal sins one can formulate a theory of neurosis and the overall theory of all of them explains many things, when one devotes oneself to following the chains of causality that enlace one's everyday experiences with one or another of these motivational roots. Aside from the fact that psychology and especially therapeutic experience have recognized the importance of what are called 'cardinal sins' in the explanation of suffering, the recent application of the psychology of enneatypes to psychotherapy has been so enthusiastically valued by therapists of different schools as to remove any doubt that these have served to make them better therapists. In addition, the formulation of characters as proposed by the psychology of enneatypes is at the same time coherent with *The Diagnostic and Statistical Manual of Mental Disorders* (DSM-V), of the American Psychiatric Association and furthermore, many agree that it is the most satisfactory explanation of personalities known to date.

I will not stop now to dwell on any specific sin, but instead consider the common nature of all of them, which is a combination of greed, destructiveness, and false love. When people say that someone is a "passionate" person, they allude with that statement to a certain excess of love that is not exactly that but instead a badly understood love by which that person can come to asphyxiate his or her beloved, control, dominate, and even kill such person. People kill because of jealousy or possessiveness, they kill because of wanting to get this or that from the other, in such a way that these sins are in reality passions, which are in turn forms of voraciousness, forms of what Maslow called *deficiency needs*, in which one does not live from one's being (a situation comparable to the water that fills a fountain and overflows) but from what lacks: living as if we were moved by a desire to fill a void in the center of ourselves.

Despite this deficiency need that fuels our lives during our immaturity, there nonetheless lies within us the potential for a psycho spiritual transformation that will bring us from a voracious state to an abundant state. Like butterflies that during their larval state as worms eat a lot, we are leeches (as was said), great devourers. Freud affirmed in his highly pessimistic vision of human nature that we are also latent parricides and cannibals. But the adult state of the human being resembles the butterflies that fly, free now of so many passionate excesses and the path is that of a purification that begins with self-awareness. While it is true that the world is moved by those old sins, which include the exaggerated search for pleasure or power, the vanity of self-importance, which relies so much on money and on other things like the need to accumulate due to anxieties about the future, it is also true that since ancient times this path of transformation has been known, which begins with the recognition of our lacks and deepens with the cultivation of virtuous attitudes.

It is just that the ancient remedies, so well-known in the Middle Ages, are now no longer so easy to apply in our time, as in the world of business, all the sins are needed, and virtue does not have a good reputation today. There is no market for virtue and a proposal of our becoming more virtuous runs the risk of seeming ridiculous because just as we do not know what wisdom is, we no longer understand what it means to be virtuous. Working against this is the fact that moral history, especially in the Western world, is the history of moralism and not of virtue. When independence was proclaimed by the United States and their constitution written, the group of people who drew up that document perceived with notable clarity that the government, through the laws that they proposed as an alternative to the old monarchic regime, could only work if the people were virtuous. However, it seems that they were not concerned with the search for virtue, since they took for granted that they themselves (Puritan English pioneers who had come in search of the creation of a better world) were very well intentioned and virtuous. Moreover, the church would take care of virtue and they trusted that the church would continue to do its good job. Looking back at the events of that time period, the "moralism" of the Puritans seems rather like a caricature to us now, because with the perspective of time we realize that they did not consider black people to be humans. They were considered to be like animals and thus could be sold and enslaved. Such an attitude did not seem immoral to them, because how could one demand moral conduct from someone with regard to a "person" who is not human? They were even further away from an environmental awareness that could lead them to respect nature and the notion that this could also have rights. The ethical position of the indigenous people seems better to us, since it could be said of them that they were implicitly Franciscans, they loved the fish, trees, and the birds and treated them as brothers. Such feeling goes much further beyond the utilitarianism that urges us to take care of scarce resources. It is based instead on empathy, by which the relationship of the subject with the object is one of *from me to you*, as Marin Buber said: a relationship that humanizes the other and humanizes even the trees. Our scientific culture, which is the modern expression of our shrewd, hunter mind, does not know how to do that.

If we must overcome our destructive passions through the development of our virtue, we must above all distinguish between the ethics of the authoritarian moral and an ethic of virtue.

By virtue, I mean something similar to Lao Tsé, the legendary founder of Taoism, who called his celebrated Tao Te Ching the "Book of the Tao and of Virtue." Although the word Tao is literally translated as "the way" and also as "nature," it alludes to cosmic law, to the deepest part of the mind, to the supreme truth and origin of everything. The word Te, which completes the title of the book, corresponds to "virtue" and refers to the virtue of those who are on the same wavelength as cosmic law. Alternatively, the title of this classic of Taoism is also translated as "The Book of Tao and Its Virtue," which already communicates the basic notion that virtue flows naturally from the harmony of the individual with the Tao. It is enough for us to be profoundly ourselves, being in harmony with the universal laws, to make what we do virtuous, to follow the Tao is all that is needed for what we do to be beneficial. This is a very different concept from extrinsic morality, with its precepts or laws that dictate what is good and what is not, or moral norms that are of the same nature as that of the laws, given that they are authoritarian views and underneath imply a political system that permeates all the ethics of the Western world.

Many therapists understand our mission as a way of helping people to free themselves from the police they carry within their heads and for them to discover that they do not need an internal police regime. What is more: if one learns to live without an internal guard or persecutor, the result is better and not worse. Despite the fact that we have been indoctrinated through our upbringing and education with the idea that our spontaneous desires are not good, it is worth learning to trust in our feelings and in our bodies, coming to see ourselves as pleasing animals and not that disgusting crocodile that psychoanalysis invites us to think lies enchained in the basement of its psychological system.

A North American semanticist, George Lakoff, says that we live with a supposition that he calls the model of the strict father, which entails the hypothesis that the best remedy for all ills is a firm hand. If the child does not study enough, daddy must be called to punish him; if students do not perform well enough, they need to be given stricter tests and those who fail will be prevented from finding jobs; if citizens do not behave well, they must be sent to jail and if it is not enough to send them to jail, then there is also the death penalty. There are those who favor the death penalty, who are also in favor of more punitive justice, despite the fact that we well know that understanding and love work better than punishment and threats. However, the punishing and threatening attitude predominates in our society (from the family to politics) and it is barely conceivable that people could live in a virtuous fashion without the control of law and the police.

There was a time when moralist ethics worked relatively well and people only lost faith in it when, through a greater sophistication, they recognized the intrinsically punitive nature of moralism. I think that today we are realizing how well formulated that myth of the fall of man after eating of the fruit of good and evil was. The Biblical texts say that we imagined that we became like gods with that great knowledge of good and evil but in reality, it is better for humans not to assume the power of judging what is good and what is bad. When we become judges of good and evil, we become moralists, and it is enough for us to propose being good or establishing generosity as an obligation for a spirit of rebellion to be born within us.

But who has faith that we can live according to an organismic intelligence? Who trusts in the intelligence of their animal nature? Collectively, we have criminalized not just the animal but also implicitly, pleasure. When Freud invites us to remember in our inner world a "pleasure principle" and a "reality principle" and suggests that we becomes mature beings when we realize that we must accept the limitations that reality puts on pleasure, I do not think that he took into account that what he is calling *reality* is in fact, only the reality of the patriarchal world; that is to say, the reality of a society in which pleasure has been condemned over millennia.

As far back as the dawn of civilization we turned against nature, not just as something to exploit in the external world but also against people and against the nature within ourselves, by treating ourselves like beasts of burden; in other words, as resources or means to certain ends that are not very human, such as ambition or profit: selfish or neurotic goals, which have to do with feeling better in our essentially lacking condition. Insomuch as this turning against what is natural in our nature and in that of our fellows is already a loss of virtue, mental health becomes that which most resembles the virtue spoken of by the ancients like Lao Tsé and also the Greeks like Socrates, or Aristotle with his *eudaimonia*, which was something like a pleasurable serenity, a state of feeling good from which good naturally followed.

Thus, the idea of morality that we now know as the therapeutic field is that which comes closest to the morality that interested the Greek and Roman moralists like the Stoics, the Epicureans, and the Cynics (and all those philosophers who came after Socrates and concerned themselves more with how one should live than the questions we now call scientific, like Marcus Aurelius, Epictetus, or Cicero). Those philosophers were people who focused on the mind and on how we should act with others, showing people how to live better. If we wish to recover virtue, we need to have an education that is not more moralistic but instead more therapeutic, which centers itself on wellbeing.

The fact that the fields of our institutions differ greatly is an obstacle for this: one thing is education (it is thought) and another is psychotherapy. It is said that one discipline should not intrude on the other; because in addition there is competition in everything, as if between two political parties or in soccer. As the dominant mentality is hegemonic, every piece of territory justifies itself and educators do not usually want psychologists to come and stick their noses into their field. However, it turns out to be very costly for education not to pay attention to happiness or good relationships between people. When a student has serious learning problems, he is sent to the educational psychologist, but the relevance of emotional development is not recognized as a basic function of educational institutions. It is absurd that in the era of Google and Wikipedia education is so concerned with information, that it ignores human development.

Now it is time to explain another *theory of neurosis* that I have been trying to implicitly propose in suggesting that the answer to the classic sins of Christianity should not just be detached neutrality but instead the virtue intrinsic to mental health. I refer to a point of view regarding suffering that appeared with Freud. The creator of psychoanalysis formulated many theories but the landscape underlying Freudian thought lies in the idea of collective castration.

Freud denounced the criminalization of instinct and especially the criminalization of desire. The Freudian vision is permeated by the idea that we are animals: let us not delude ourselves with too many tales of our spiritual nature, Freud seemed to tell us. Let us begin by accepting that we are also animals and that as such, we are very discontent in the cage in which we find ourselves. The civilization that we have created is anti-erotic and repressive. That civilization educates us to not trust in pleasure, as well as to place reason above all other things: reason and its authority; duty above pleasure. Civilization is in a certain way just that: the choice of duty over pleasure. That is how the warrior code of ancient peoples explicitly formulated it. A warrior could let himself be pierced by an arrow without a murmur, because the warrior spirit dictated that the spirit controls the body and that intellect rules over conduct, through the orders of duty. The Japanese are capable of taking their own lives by stabbing themselves in the belly with a knife when their code of honor so demands, and that implies a heroic ideal embodied in people capable of going beyond their basic instincts.

It is true that there is something within us that goes beyond the body, but I do not think an education anchored in the compulsive disdain of the body and desire is useful. The price of unhappiness is very high and the revenge of instinct when it is not satisfied consists of its transforming into many phantasmagoric things, like neurotic desires and destructive *passions*.

Freud lived under the influence of Nietzsche and surely learned more from Nietzsche than from his masters in the world of physiology, neurology, or medicine. Nietzsche thought that the fossilized Christianity of his time needed an injection of Dionysian spirit. What was the Dionysian spirit for Nietzsche? In part, a faith in nature. If there are animal desires in us, they are comparable to the tropisms of plants, which know how to send their roots down where there is water or to turn their flowers toward the sun. It does not occur to us to criminalize such actions of plants; just as it does not occur to us that thirst, hunger, or sexual desire are perversions in animals. We do not control animals and it would be laughable to want to control the sex lives of dogs and cats: luckily for them we do not get so involved in their lives. Luckily for us, the mental health of cats helps us, just as that of horses or dolphins. There are cats and dogs that greatly help their owners to survive in depressive moments or moments of alienation.

If what Freud suggests in stating that we are very unhappy animals in the cage of our civilized life is true, then Nietzsche's proposal that we cultivate a spirit of greater permissiveness would be very good: greater appreciation and less criminalization of desires. That is what William Reich, who believed even more than Freud in liberation from the repressive forces of society in order to remove the animal from its cage or prison, took forward. An educator inspired by Reich, A.S. Neill, created the famous Summerhill School, an experiment in permissiveness and love, inspired by the idea that what is most important in education is precisely freedom and love. Many happy people emerged from that school, but very bad things were said of Summerhill. These venomous tongues had more weight than the scientific information based on longitudinal studies and scandal was unleashed in the community, so much so that some of the parents of the children at Summerhill became very concerned that their children were being raised in such a free environment. Something similar took place again in the 1960s, when the countercultural movement was born. The authorities were frightened by the possible social consequences of young people who took drugs and were judging so critically their well-intentioned parents and grandparents. A generation gap was produced: such an enormous abyss between one generation and the next, that politicians chose to demonize the youth.

Many revolutionary initiatives had already arisen in the 1960s in California, which was the Mecca of this movement: environmentalism, the new feminism, the civil liberties movement, a new therapeutic inspiration and especially a great movement of spiritual searching; thus, when correctly perceiving that if young people prevailed they would no longer have an easily manipulated society, the authorities decided to intervene and put into action a new conservatism that has dominated in the world until today. In this time a deliberate youth criminalization movement began and as a part of this, drugs were also criminalized, which were associated with the supposedly dangerous juvenile mentality that does not heed the authorities. Similar to how everything was blamed on the Jews in Germany, this movement tried to make the public feel that youth, with their counterculture and their drugs, had become the great danger that threatened America. This criminalization was a very well-orchestrated movement, especially regarding what is called the "war on drugs," which did not arise from a medical concern for the health of people (no matter how many false experiments were published that supposedly proved the chromosomal damage caused by LSD) but instead was a secretly political war, based on the fear of awareness and liberation.

It is embarrassing that the war against drugs continues

today, in the veritable boom of economic crimes that are killing so many people and moreover, so many more than could conceivably die from the consumption of drugs. Why such ferocity? It seems to me that it is just because some people have understood that the awakening of consciousness has a political implication, preventing people from being like a flock able to be manipulated by school or television and conformity. The same drugs that benefited the religious lives of the ancient peoples and could today benefit psychotherapy, can also lead to a *dangerous* wisdom.

I have touched on this subject of the repressive spirit and the need for a more permissive culture and to it I bring Freud's insight on turning against natural desires. If it is a fact that permissiveness, whether this is in the educational field or in upbringing, that awakens so much social scandal, what can we do to reach a healthier culture?

Perhaps, the primary impasse lies in the fact that when children do not honor that Biblical mandate to love and respect their father and mother so that life becomes uncomfortable for the parents, and few among them know how to receive the criticisms of their children. Even when parents recognize their imperfections, that does not mean that they are willing to let their children be the ones who call their faults to their attention, because for parents to be able to learn from their children requires an uncommonly advanced state of awareness.

Some say that there are children being born who come to show us how to evolve; children who are increasingly wiser, with the mission of not paying much attention to the ideals of their parents and therefore sweeping away the suppositions and ideologies, preparing us for a very different world. Whatever the case may be, it would be worth at least recognizing that society's repressive forces are part of the evil and therefore part of the problem; it is worth keeping clear that what we call civilization is the establishment of a repressive culture. We all know very well now that in the establishment of an intrinsically repressive patriarchal society, there was authoritarianism from the very start, so that the things that are happening now are not *complications* of civilization but instead manifestations of ancient contradictions that no longer prove sustainable for us.

Let me continue with the Freudian vision of neurosis. As psychoanalysis and later psychotherapy in general began to evolve, it began to be discovered that people suffer not just because their instinctive nature has been shackled but also from wounds of love; because of a "Lovesickness" that began when as children, their need for love was frustrated. It could be said that just as in an epidemic that is transmitted from generation to generation, from parents to children and then to grandchildren, frustrated love is passed on, in such a way that we cannot be as supportive with our children as we (and they themselves) might like us to be, seeing that we fall short in giving them the attention they need. We are occupied with too many things and in particular with achieving the love we lacked in our own childhood, since to achieve that love we must do many things that are contrary to our own nature.

Some people, to achieve love, try to be perfect, others become excessively courteous, and there are people who in order to obtain love invent imaginary suffering, believing themselves to be more unhappy than they are. We have many different ways, according to our nature, and there are those who need to feel they are gratifying all their desires in order to feel loved and therefore cannot bear frustration. The need for love is a great plague. I think that we can all discover this addiction to love within ourselves, which makes the Japanese so astonished that we are so obsessed with romantic love.

What we have not discovered, however, is that our obsession for love prevents us from being more loving. Mental health is a happy state that relies on us exercising our potential to love; when one is giving loving, one is happy, whether this is loving a person, enjoying a work of music, defending justice, or taking care of a child. There are many forms of love.

It would seem that the cure for the need for love would be to simply recover over the course of our adult lives that which we lacked in the past. However, to obtain the love that we did not have is not just very difficult but in fact, when we do obtain it, this does not help very much. It has some use, because when one is being loved, one can love but this does not last long and we already know that the happiness of love is fleeting. Even though some persist in loving us, the infatuation loses its freshness, which is not a definitive solution.

To recover from lovesickness, one must love. In order to be able to love, it is not necessary to invent a fake identity or to construct a capacity for love that we do not have; since our very essence is loving and the problem is just that because of being angry and sick, our loving quality has become blocked.

One type of love that exists in all of us is enjoyment. It is a kind of loving emotion and no one would doubt that we all aspire to experience enjoyment. We are all born with a capacity for enjoyment, but we have lost it. People have a limited capacity for enjoyment and there are those who suffer much better than they enjoy; or they stubbornly insist on suffering: it is as if they get more mileage out of the tears of suffering, than those of joy.

Charitable love is not so easy, because who knows how to forgive? Our conditioned psychic apparatus, which acts like a machine, functions in a very resentful way in reaction to frustrations and offences and we take revenge much more easily than we can forgive. To forgive is like emerging beyond the psychological machine, it is like going beyond our limits. We could say that forgiveness is a spiritual act that arises from going within the other and taking pity on their needs, also understanding that it is better when one forgives, both for the other as well as for oneself. But it is difficult to take that step.

Nonetheless, methods to do so exist in current psychotherapy, although education has not turned to them until now, unfortunately, given that if we wish to be consistent with the ideals of "Western Christian Civilization," nothing would be more important than drawing on such methods, since only a person who enters through the door of forgiveness can walk the *path of love.* To go beyond resentment is something difficult to do without someone who has already lived that process leading us by the hand. Some contemporary therapists already know how to do that rather well, but the educators do not concern themselves with this, not considering it part of their responsibility.

Therefore, as it is important that we develop the compassionate or empathetic love that we derive from maternal love, it is important for us to develop another kind of love that aims at the ideal and which derives from the child's ties with the figure of the father. The father is, for the little child, the person to whom the mother looks and therefore is a point of reference. Although the child has little contact with the father, he represents something like the mother hen for the little chicks that follow it: an order of values. In a dying patriarchal world like the one we live in, we have lost the love of 'fathers of the fatherland', of the 'fathers of the Church' and even of the father of the home, which until recently was a figure of great authority. The worth of the father has decreased a lot and in children's later lives this translates into a loss of values; we no longer admire nor respect much, nor do we look upward, and it is a case of repairing that loss of values with an education for values. However current education in values is one based on sermons: "How beautiful is beauty" some say and others: "But honesty is very honest!" They glorify each of the values but the attempts to help ourselves to be more just or caring through the beauty of the sermons does not replace the healthy development of an admiring love that, like compassion or enjoyment, is an intrinsic faculty of our essence. Call it love of the ideal, of the divine, or simply devotion. It is a freely given love; it has to do with contemplation and also with the intuition of our potential and the motivation of leading us to its realization.

I say all this because, as incredible as it might seem, the cure for lovesickness from which our species suffers so much lies not in the intensification of our thirst for love or in the attempt to buy love doing all sorts of things that end up alienating us.

The happiness of the love that deep down we are looking for is not found when we want it but when we manage to become more loving, realizing the potential of our nature. However, it would be difficult to educate our descendants to love their neighbors or to love life without beginning with something more elemental: loving ourselves.

Believing erroneously that we already love ourselves, we do not have any idea of how much we in fact hate, persecute, torture, and underestimate ourselves. Without the basis of this love for ourselves, it is only with difficulty that we can reach that love of others, which is a phenomenon of overflow. Loving God could be easier, since He is perfect; but we humans have so many defects.

Devotion is already obsolete, we no longer believe in it; moreover, we already have problems collectively with the father figure. Nonetheless, the root of devotion is appreciative love, a love that looks upward and that can be educated independently of beliefs. One can educate in admiring love through music, for example. Listening to Beethoven's *Eroica* symphony, or seeing the Sistine Chapel, are experiences that we call sublime because they involve that capacity of looking to the heavens, which is like the contrast to compassionate love that looks to the earth or to human beings.

I think that the Greeks were correct when they said that in terms of education it was enough to go to the gymnasium for the body and listen to music for the soul and that true education was the province and responsibility of the legislators.

Thus, on contemplating how today we must live in a society that turns us into egotists, makes us sick and corrupts us, we can understand the importance of constructing a world in which people can develop themselves well.

Now it would seem that we live under an economic dictatorship where those who govern us obey the laws of money and the dictates of the global empire of commerce and it would seem that there is no space for anything other than money and politics. In any case, all the things that we have been discussing as relevant considerations for the evolution of our consciousness are precisely the most irrelevant for our legislation and institutions.

If one examines what our response would rationally be if we took into consideration the causes of suffering in the world, one would realize that we need people who are wiser, more aware and more loving who, being more loving, would also be more virtuous and being better human beings, they would make up the basis of a happier society. Is it possible to create healthy tissue without healthy cells?

However, it turns out that talking about these things is almost forbidden; because to talk of love in an academic environment or in an educational institution is the equivalent of not being scientific or academic; that is to say: of using the 'wrong brain'. Nonetheless, it is the sum of such things that would make up a *politics of consciousness*, and the apparent irrelevance of all that makes evident that today a *politics of unconsciousness* reigns, from which standpoint nothing written about here is education, or even good or relevant.

I have not finished examining the theories of the neurosis and we have yet to consider what is sometimes called *existential theory*. It originally arose in psychoanalysis and it was said that certain people have a "weak self," which means that some suffer because they are searching for themselves but do not succeed. It seems to me that if there are only few who suffer because of not finding themselves, that is because only few come to search for themselves. In reality, we have all lost our souls but few of us are called to find it again. In other words, only few people discover their apparent inexistence and realize that Descartes' famous aphorism is no more than reasoning. Who knows they exist, in addition to thinking about it? Very few. Perhaps, the more we think, the less we experientially verify our existence and perhaps it would be more correct to say: "I don't think, therefore I am," because it is much easier to feel our immediate existence when we do not distract ourselves from our immediate experience with our thinking.

The feeling of existence, in other words, the feeling that one is, is not a function of thought, as a result of which the Cartesian argument has been called into question by phenomenologists like Paul Ricoeur. "I think, therefore I am" is a logical thought and few realize its fallacy. It is said that people become sick when they do not find themselves, but I think that what happens is in fact the opposite: only deep people realize that they do not exist and that it is true that *we do not exist*. Or, said another way, existence is a state of being at which we have not arrived. It would be more legitimate to say that instead of fooling ourselves thinking that *we are*, we should think: "When I get older, I shall be." Because only when one reaches maturity can the pleasure of knowing one exists be found.

There are various levels of explanation of the fact that we lack perception of our own selves, no matter how much evidence we have of our physical, emotional, and cognitive perceptions. The psychoanalytical explanation is that we are disintegrated; we are not one, and only a whole or unified person can feel a "self." A machine, which is a sum of separate parts, cannot have a united consciousness. If our thinking is dissociated from our feeling and our desires make up a world apart, where is the part that says, "I am"?

Some neurophysiologists, or neurobiologists or cognitivists as they are now called, say that the synthesis between our psychic regions is a function of the prefrontal cortex. I remember having heard Daniel Siegel describe the case of a woman who had a developed a lesion on her prefrontal cortex, who continued doing everything she had done before, but her children said: "It's as if our mother had lost her soul." She was missing something intangible and that had made her seem more like a zombie than a person as such. She could think, she could go shopping, and she could even pay attention to her children, but it was as if she were missing the most vital element that had made her human: that function of synthesizing all parts of herself.

It is as if we were a triangular pyramid. We have three brains, it is sometimes said: the intellectual and properly human brain, which is the neocortex; the middle brain, emotional or relational, that we have in common with other mammals; and the instinctive or reptilian brain. However, these three brains, which should be harmonized by a process of synthesis, seem not to function in the majority of people, except in a very partial way.

This idea moved me deeply through two influences: one being Gurdjieff, spiritual master born at the end of the 19th century in Georgia, like Stalin, and who became known in Russia just before the Bolshevik Revolution to later emigrate, first to Turkey and then to France. There he founded a school that is called the Institute for the Harmonious Development of Man and he already spoke of the three brains, although Paul McLean had not yet formulated that idea through his studies of the evolution of the brain. Through the voice of his character Beelzebub (who travels in a spaceship that leads him through the center of the universe once his mission is completed and explains to his grandson the problems of the unfortunate inhabitants of the planet Earth), Gurdjieff states that humans suffer because they cannot coordinate their three brains. He also explains the human condition through the analogy of a horse-drawn car driven by a coachman. The car is like the body, and the driver, naturally, is the intellect–which knows how to get to this or that street avoiding obstacles. The horse represents our emotional, or motivational aspect but after explaining this analogy, Gurdjieff adds that we are like rental cars that do not carry the passenger for whom they were destined. At different moments of our lives we follow different influences and we place ourselves in the service of this or that but deep down, we feel the emptiness due to absence of the passenger for whom this carriage was built. Let us call it the 'self', or the 'true self', the 'essence', the terminology is secondary. What is important is to realize that we do not have a stable self, rather we call our momentary experiences *self*. From the realization of the illusory nature of our self, a *true self* can arise, in the first place because from such a realization it is natural that there emerges an aspiration and from an aspiration, the encounter with who we are deep down, the motivation for a relevant practice. Particularly relevant is that which makes up the most important aspect of its education and what he called *self-remembering*: a concentration on the sense of existence, beyond mental phenomena.

A similar practice is found in the teachings of Ramana Maharshi, who established as a fundamental practice the experiential investigation of the question: "Who am I?" A question which has at the same time its equivalent in the development of intrinsic awareness.

If we have forgotten the experience of being to such a degree that we do not get very far in our attempt to remember it, we can yearn for it from our *existential void.* That yearning for being–inseparable from the yearning for the divine–is already devotion, or at least the root of devotion, beyond its ritualized forms through prayer and the concentration on sacred symbols such as mantras, divine names, etc. Therefore, the very awareness of forgetting our being is already a painful aspiration to awakening, and a stimulus for our search.

Finally, the idea that the loss of the experience of the "I am" is due to psychic disintegration is a very productive point of view, as it indicates the relevance and importance of the resolution of intra-psychic conflicts, which are intricately tied to family conflicts.

A contemporary of Gurdjieff, Tótila Albert, who had the good fortune to meet him personally and who was another of my important influences when I was young, talks about this. He was known in Chile as a sculptor, but was more a wise man than an artist, and primarily, I would say, a prophet. He was the first critic of patriarchal society and nothing motivated him more than awakening his fellows to the aberration of the world and the need for a new world that was based on a balance between the father, the mother, and the child; not just on a family level, but also on an intra-psychic one and on the world of cultural values.

Bachofen, who had become interested in the matriarchies

of some ancient peoples, had already implicitly discovered the patriarchal bias of our society but he had idealized it, presenting it as a step forward in the evolution of culture (as has usually been done when thinking of the birth of civilization as a simple progress) associated with writing, the calendar, large urban centers, and temples. Then came the archaeologists, who showed that with the patriarchal society came the origins of inequalities and injustices, slavery, wars, and many evils, so that it was not only 'good' that entered into the world when women were subjugated–the emotional or empathetic world was also subjugated. With the crushing of women, children remained unprotected against the supposedly natural despotism of their fathers, thereby losing the most dialogical relationship of the *primitives*, who loved their children more, and considered them more when making decisions.

If we understand psychic suffering as an inner emptiness caused by disintegration, we must concern ourselves not only with understanding our intra-psychic situation but also with developing an aspiration to resolve our inner conflicts between reason, emotion and instinct, as well as between our paternal and potentially aggressive aspect, our empathetic maternal aspect and that part of us that is not only our inner child but also our inner animal: our natural self before our cultural conditioning.

Tótila Albert's approach also includes a vision that we could characterize as a systematic theory of neurosis.

If what we call "civilization" is a world in which the father has dominated the mother and child, we could say that the origin of our personal neurosis (with the fact that our brains cannot operate together) is a sort of cultural contamination. In a world in which people lie, in which no voice is given to what children feel (they barely have the right to feel let alone to say what they feel), little by little they begin to lose the right to feel what they feel. R.D. Laing spoke of a *politics of experience*: a repressive politics with regard to experience, a taboo of awareness itself.

Tótila Albert embraced a social vision according to which the alternative to patriarchy is not matriarchy, with its return to matristic values, but according to his view of history, we had lived above all a filiarchy before we became sedentary. Like animals, we were anarchic and this governing of the individual by himself seems to have been functional until the experience of hunger during the last ice age made us cannibals (as the broken skulls of some of our Neanderthal ancestors suggest). Then governing by the community over the individual was established, the matristic government, the primitive communist government, that we can imagine as a tyrannical group. It seems that in that Neolithic era, which we associate with ceramics and textiles, not just the arts emerged but also religion, or what we call the spirit. Culture emanated and it seems that it would have been a step forward. Then came central government, despotic, the authoritarian and patriarchal government and it seems that it would have been functional initially, having been necessary in a time of great drought. The community needed to be moved, it needed to be organized and we had to become hunters again to survive. All religions keep the memory of this in the consecration of sacrifices; there is no religion that does not have sacrifices. Why sacrifices? It is as if we had wanted to keep a historic memory that killing is sometimes holy because it is inevitable; to defend life one has to kill. Killing animals was already tragic for people who lived so closely to them and then, to kill humans.

We became barbarians. Civilization was born of barbarism when the hunters of animals became hunters of people, cascading down upon the sedentary peoples who were a little more civilized, on the banks of the great rivers.

Unlike those who conceive of the alternative to patriarchy as a return to the matristic world, Tótila Albert's concept was what he called literally the "three times ours" (our three inner selves, in implicit reference to the Lord's Prayer): a world in which not only are the three interpretations of the divine in balance as the Father, Mother, and Child but one in which the power is also balanced. If, in view of the abuses on the part of despotic governments, there are those who had dreamed of a world without government, someone who has worked in group psychotherapy can see that a little authority greatly accelerates the process of self-organization. I think it is true that, as Tótila thought, we need the three principles (paternal, maternal, and filial) that correspond with our three brains. Therefore, it seems to me that the political alternative to the patriarchal order would be an equilibrium between self-governance of the people, the sense of community, and the central government. The social order would not then be hierarchic, but instead heterarchical.

But how can all this be made reality, when everything I am talking about is so irrelevant to the current political world? If one wanted an alternative world to become a reality, the training of people to be more generous, more aware, more virtuous would be a priority. How difficult all that would be given the immense population of the present world and the fact that people are not primarily interested in being helped to change.

Then, why do I talk of these quixotic ideas, so apparently devoid of a sense of reality? Because the world is crumbling and civilization has entered a critical phase, in which this artificial system we have constructed is becoming growingly dysfunctional and even catastrophic; and because, in addition, people are recognizing the pathology of the system. Already virtually no one believes that the governments are especially representative or trustworthy.

Given such a state of affairs I have become a little apocalyptic; I understand the word *apocalypse* as 'revelation' and I think that the revelation consists of realizing what exists, how things are. Is that not what is happening? It seems that, for the first time, people are seeing the face of the beast that has always been there—for *the Beast* is none other than the spirit of civilization.

The Romans identified the "Great Beast" with Rome, just as the Jews had seen the crushing evil of the great civilizations they had survived: first Egypt and then Babylonia. The Metropolis is the beast with which we have lived, beyond its forms: the patriarchal order itself that we have exalted as *civilization*, with its monopoly of power and its slow degradation over the centuries and millennia.

In the times of counterculture, for the first time we glimpsed the perversion of the system that rules us, once again people are becoming aware of their blindness and impotency and they are indignant. It is in the face of this that I voice this advice that I once heard a Sufi say in response to what should be done with the ego and which I have reproduced at the start of this book.

Should the ego, the neurosis, that part of us that is so narcissistic and so desiring to be the center of everything that is not our true self and against which we fight to become ourselves, be destroyed? Should it be transformed? Or instead is it a case of simply changing our relationship with the ego, as happens in the case of someone who mounts a horse and subsequently has it at their service?

I no longer need to repeat the joke that I told in my introduction and it is enough to remind my readers of its conclusion: "It falls away by itself!"

It seems to me that our hope is that just as the most destructive aspects of our personality can lose their power over us when, understanding them completely, they start to seem comical to us, perhaps also in our collective life a process of abandonment and disintegration of the obsolete and the ineffective is beginning to take place, which leaves space for a regeneration of new ways of life and institutions.

It is often repeated in our critical time that in the I Ching, the ideogram for crisis juxtaposes the characters with the meaning of 'Danger' and 'Opportunity'. The word crisis comes from medicine, where it alludes to the moment in the development of an illness in which it becomes apparent whether the patient will get better or die. All of this is perfectly applicable to our time, in which we cannot conceive of survival without a profound transformation, given the unsustainability of our collective way of life.

It is better for us to face our crisis as an opportunity, beyond its dangers and disasters. How will people be fed when the commercial or transport companies no longer work? When the economic system no longer works, will we need to go back to barter, or will we create an alternative currency to that of banks and governments? Perhaps, in letting loose our catastrophic imagination, we do not manage to calculate the opportunity for the community to self-organize according to its own creativity, or we are not keeping in mind the degree to which we know how to do this better than our outdated institutions, once they leave us free to act.

I think that it falls to the youth of today to build a new world and it will need to be built from the personal world, from consciousness, paying attention to childrearing, education, the media, and culture to encourage awareness. In the development of the Western world, we have not believed in awareness: we can already understand how destructive it has been to forget about it; or even more, the conspiracy against it: a war of the system against the possibility of us becoming too aware.

CHAPTER 2

From Inner Poverty to Multifaceted Spirituality

I N THE PREVIOUS CHAPTER, I have examined a series of interpretations about the fundamental causes of suffering and through the analysis of each of them, there has emerged an implicit list of corollaries to those views of our problems. Or, expressed another way, a series of antidotes to our ills: the *wisdom* that opposes our blindness; the *stillness* or inner peace, that we have considered as the antidote to our disproportionately uneasy minds, moved by excessive desires and aversions; the *empathetic love* or solidarity, which would be the answer to our chronic suffering due to a lack of love, as well as to the conflicts of our selfish society; the *devotion*, through which we become aware of our inner emptiness and of our search for meaning; our *submission* to the current of life, which would also require us to heed our healthy instinctiveness and would cure the complications of our repressive culture; *self-awareness*, that would let us triumph over our specters and irrational ideas; *attention* to the experience of the moment, indispensable for self-awareness and that *delving deeper* into the experience of the present that could lead us to the contact with our fundamental self, beyond identification with our neurotic needs.

The impression the statement leaves us with, that these antidotes are the solutions to our suffering (and not just to our individual suffering but to that of our problematic world) is one that could seem excessively idealistic, utopian, or theoretical, in view of the distance between the ordinary human condition and those inner states. The fact of there being so much distance between our current reality and our desired condition is also something that could be described as a situation of great inner poverty in the world, a badly recognized inner poverty, which has come to enormously complicate the material poverty so visible to the majority.

It is because the concrete misery of the masses who do not have food to eat or clean water to drink or fire to warm themselves is so visible and the consequences of these lacks so serious in terms of illness, death, violence, destructiveness, crime and greed, that we pay little attention to the impoverishment of people's inner lives. People who, in their slavery to earn their daily bread, do not have enough free time to take care of the more subtle things, so that it ends up appearing that the subtler things, like quality of life, are superfluous.

Are we really in the world only to eat and reproduce, or does human existence respond to a purpose that in our collective ignorance we have forgotten? I will not try to argue about that but will merely express that it seems to me that practically *all of humanity has come to live meaningless lives*. If this does not lead to mass suicides it is because a *large part of humanity has lost the awareness of their unawareness*, becoming so robotic that they are not even capable of asking what they truly want from their lives.

It also seems to me that inner poverty, like certain infectious plagues, does not distinguish between the poor and the rich, but infects everyone. Unquestionably, inner poverty can be as present in the lives of the rich as in those of the poor; among whom certain human values such as generosity or devotion abound (although perhaps unconsciously) more than among those who live lives revolving around exploitation and greed. Unawareness is just as contagious as awareness.

The theme of a hero who opposes the forces of evil is common in many works of science fiction and children's comics and said forces are generally characterized as being highly intelligent. In a similar fashion, the *systematic igno-*

rance in which we live strikes us as highly intelligent. In other words: if we understand the world, as in myths, in terms of an opposition between the forces of light and darkness, we must not underestimate the intelligence of the darkness; an intelligence that transcends that of the people who live in society.

Let us consider our situation in the modern world from a panoramic view. We primarily come into to the world through a technological birth, usually a cesarean. Even in relatively poor countries like Brazil, more than 43 percent of people are born via cesarean (70 percent in the private health system) despite the fact that less than one percent really requires this operation. A few decades ago, it was enough for children to be born in the presence of midwives, women who knew how to help during childbirth since time immemorial and who, when I studied medicine, did so better than the obstetricians, whose mission was instead to attend to those emergencies that required surgery. Nonetheless, during the course of a few decades, the interests of the surgeons have prevailed over the simple but effective gifts of the midwives, who today are not accepted by law unless they have been trained (or rather indoctrinated) in a school of nursing.

Is it not an aberration that a woman cannot, in today's

day and age, give birth as she desires? Is not what the medical profession prescribes with its customs and opinions an invasion of her life and body? The more we know about the human mind, the more we understand the damage that a technological birth brings with it, in which the natural rhythms are interrupted, artificial substances are injected, the umbilical cord is prematurely severed, the backs of newborns are patted in such a way that spinal micro-hemorrhages are formed that lead to many deaths (until recently of unknown causes) and the babies are separated from their mothers, as if this were simply a case of putting distance between one object and another.

The difference between the psyche of a newborn in our culture and another in African culture can be appreciated by the fact that the first recognized reflex in the human being, which is that of smiling at the mother's face, usually appears on the third day of life in the civilized world, whereas among the Africans it usually appears immediately at birth, since their consciousness was never dulled by anesthetics, nor was the continuity of the psychic union of the child with the mother ever disturbed.

Lately, an alternative movement has arisen in the world that defends natural births, and which argues in favor of these in consideration of the wellbeing of the newborns themselves. Beyond the wellbeing of those who are born, are we not already contributing to a sick society through this technological power that collectively disembowels us from natural birth? It is as if the system were imposing, despotically, that all of us on being born place our faith in technology more than in nature. We are all born anguished and crying, we probably felt at the moment of being born that we were dying, and we have probably become weaker, so that all the blows of life have made us implicitly remember that awful original experience.

We can look at it as the result of a general insensitivity but is it not as if the spirit of the system had its own demoniacal intelligence? I imagine that when the ancients spoke of the devil, they referred to a phenomenon of this sort: an intelligence that no particular individual embodied but which seemed to impregnate all.

I have chosen just one example, but it also seems that a systemic intelligence had orchestrated for our technological births to be followed by a patriarchal upbringing, with the implicit severity of a culture that does not believe in natural impulse. Is it not perfectly logical that we are subsequently sent to school, where we end up being indoctrinated in the rejection of our spontaneous nature and our preferences, to then enter into a system of power and adopt the ideas transmitted by our educators? Our bosses will take care of the rest in the workplaces in which we end up and then television, in which enormous sums are invested to ensure that we see reality only through a filter. It is as if the world had chosen that true life be subjugated to a pseudo-life that squeezes and impoverishes it, supposedly to extract something of value from it, only what happens is precisely the opposite. Values end up becoming *goods* and inner richness, which should be a natural state of living people, becomes an artificial inner poverty which such an abundance of goods conceals so that even the poor of the world seem to have no better alternative than consumerism. The path to true richness, like inner richness itself, has become invisible.

As utopian as it seems then, what inner richness really is does not cease to be clear: a set of mental states and abilities that we could call *existential proficiencies*, to distinguish them from the current academic and labor proficiencies recognized by the educational world. Proficiencies that we should consider part of our nature but which we have let atrophy through our collective history to such a degree that it now seems difficult for us to recover them. Without them, we are not only condemned to unhappiness, but we become incapable of maintaining worthy and virtuous human relationships and of building a healthy society.

We do not just recognize these proficiencies as aspects of ourselves that we value or that establish their presence because of their insufficient development, rather it is easy to recognize that they are the key reference points in the great wisdom traditions of the world.

The Christian world is familiar above all with *love thy neighbor* and *love of God* (or devotion). In Buddhism, *attention to the here and now* and *detachment* are central. In the Dionysian religion, which preceded all the remaining religions in the Western world (and also in Taoism and Shivaism) the emphasis is placed instead on *freedom, spontaneity* and *harmony with our natural tendencies and nature itself. Self-awareness* has achieved its greatest development in the most modern field of the paths of growth: psychotherapy. And *wisdom*, so forgotten in our time, was the specialty of the Oriental spiritual schools but it was also that *truth* that the Christians of the Apostolic period knew (as well as Master Eckhart) that the Gospels say shall set us free.

We can talk of this set of existential proficiencies as the dimensions of a complete spirituality. It seems to me that the historic process through which all the spiritual legacies of the world are converging in our modern society (just as their old formulas, rites, and costumes are falling away) leads many people today to leave their old churches, to nourish themselves directly from the basic elements in the sources of this spiritual diet, which our global, cosmopolitan and multicultural world has placed within reach.

And that is how, despite the great poverty of our explicit spiritual culture, a great richness is also appearing that is present above all in the subculture of the seekers in this world: people who, moved by their *thirst to be*, partially sacrifice their comfort, safety, and advantages. It could be said that they are, without knowing it, apprentice shamans who in searching for their own development, will sooner or later have the possibility of being of help, in a world needing precisely those qualities they are developing. It seems to me that together with the wise men of different spiritual traditions, who have already undertaken a long journey to reach their wisdom, these young seekers are a great hope for our world in transformation.

CHAPTER 3

Rehumanizing Education:

BEYOND THE FINANCIAL CRISIS, INEQUALITY, AND VIOLENCE

W E ALREADY KNOW TOO WELL that we are not only going through a multifaceted crisis that is becoming more aggravated and that seems to be leading us to the collapse of our sociopolitical and economic system. Moreover, this social disaster will also coincide with a natural environment impoverished by environmental damage and global warming.

In my book *The Patriarchal Mind*, I have compared our crisis to the one from which what we call the civilized world arose some seven thousand years ago, when the warming of the Earth led to the establishment of a patriarchal society, with its characteristic hunter's violence concealed by lofty ideals.

Nevertheless, one does not need to look to prehistory nor to the origins of the civilized world to consider the analysis that I present here with regard to the nature of the social meta-problem that afflicts us. It is enough to look at the world around us to perceive the repressive nature of civilization (also amply analyzed from Freud to Foucault) and to understand that behind our many problems lie a degradation of awareness and a process of dehumanization that has accompanied our civilization process.

By proposing that the crux of the crisis of civilization that we are going through consists of a *patriarchal mind* that coexists with patriarchal society, I simply allude to a pattern of violence, insensitivity and greed that is associated with ignoring maternal empathy and bodily, animal wisdom.

I have proposed in some of my books (*Healing Civilization* and *The Patriarchal Mind*) that in addition to the patriarchal society the institution of the *paterfamilias* establishes an appropriation of womankind and children by the father, just as in our cultural world and in the inner world of most people a priority of intellect (paternal) over love (maternal) and over instinct (filial) has been established; so that, adopting the point of view of a trinitarian anthropology that defines us as tri-brained, I propose that the change of paradigm that will free us from the destructive obsolescence of the patriarchal mind will be one that orients us toward the condition of being complete or tri-unified.

It is not necessary to agree with my analysis of humans as disintegrated, tri-brained beings to agree that since our fundamental problem is our consciousness (in other words, our lack of benevolence, wisdom and freedom), it is sufficient to recognize this in order to understand that only a process of massive psycho-spiritual development could save us from our planetary crisis.

Is it not then imperative for the academic sector, immersed in its routines of instruction and research, to wake up to the urgency of human development?

Paraphrasing the opinion which is attributed to Einstein that our problems can only be solved by a mind that is different from that which created them, I would say that we can only transcend the patriarchal mind through a transformation that allows us to recover our instinctive, animal wisdom, our capacity for love and a lucidity that rescues us from our current, collective blindness, which in our all-knowing arrogance, we are not even sufficiently aware to recognize and regret.

Therefore, it seems to me that our best collective hope is that of a transformation of education and that we must without delay endeavor to train a generation that is wiser, more caring and healthier than the one we belong to and which we so arrogantly seek to reproduce through our educational institutions.

I have desired nothing more than to be heard by those people who have the power to intervene effectively toward a change in education to achieve what I have come to consider is my message, which I usually summarize with the phrase "change education to change the world." Through this, I have aimed to transmit the conviction that in view of the nature of the worldwide problem, the most important thing that we can hope for is a massive change in people's awareness and to achieve this, nothing can be more relevant than a radical and broad change of the educational system.

By "radical change" I mean a change that involves redefining education, so that this becomes able to direct itself toward a different aim than that of the traditional education in vogue, which is characterized by its emphasis on the passing on of information and on adapting people to patriarchal society, which has become an increasingly explicit problem.

Although it is true that a change or enrichment of higher education would not be enough to achieve this (since in order to rely on a generation that is healthier, freer and wiser, the transformation of secondary education would be more important), as one might imagine, the transformation of secondary education will depend on such higher education. Let us hope that primary education conserves its aspects of mothering, spontaneity and relevance to life despite the current danger that it is beginning to echo the negative aspects of secondary education.

For many years now I have been saying that we must reform the education of our educators, in such a way that we do not convert the career of school teacher into yet another of the careers taught in colleges of higher education, which neglect the human development of their trainees. No matter how desirable it would be for other professionals to be able to receive human training, such as those who devote themselves to psychotherapy and perhaps one day politicians, it is more important than anything to halt dehumanization in the training of our educators.

Naturally, I think that all departments should recover their roles in the training of human beings, not only concerning themselves with training experts in this or that specialty and that only in this way will they recover the right to call themselves a "university" as a whole. Nonetheless, it must begin with one department and nothing strikes me as more important in the pursuit of rehumanizing society than rehumanizing education (apart from the rather chimerical goal of humanizing the business world), something that not even what is known as Humanism was able to accomplish.

If education is to one day be rehumanized, I do not have the slightest doubt that it would not be enough to do so through legislation and curricular reforms; since "humanity" is transmitted through human relationships, which in this case consist of the relationships between masters and disciples. For that, the key to transforming education must be transforming those who educate the educators.

In turn, in order to transform the educators of educators (who enable them to pass on a transforming education), an efficient and possible method of financing will be essential; a method that I have drawn up during forty years of continuous exploration of a way of working with groups of seekers, therapists and teachers, which today is known as the Seekers After Truth (SAT) Program.

I suppose that finding that such programs work very well might have been an important factor in my optimism. There is something quixotic about making the proposal: "Let's change education to change the world," and I have no doubt that it has been the success and recognition of the SAT programs for which I am primarily known that has informed my optimism.

CHAPTER 4

Freedom, The Basis of Love

THERE IS MUCH TALK TODAY regarding emotional education, although the attempts to go beyond words are little more than superficial and insufficient exercises and they continue avoiding the use of the word love; which is what is truly necessary for the world in which we live (and if it is not named, contributes to the educational efforts deviation from what is truly important).

I ask myself if, perhaps, the taboo directed at the word "love" which is present in our bureaucracies is related to an implicit and unacknowledged feeling that the Christian message was of little use, or that the State should not try to follow a goal already taken on (with questionable success) by the Church.

Whatever the reason, it seems to me that the Dalai Lama is right in wandering around the world giving talks about there being nothing more important in our time than our learning to be a little kinder.

But how?

Without doubt, the sermons and good intentions of many generations to make ourselves better people have failed and something more is needed.

When tackling this subject of how we can become more empathetic, caring, brotherly and generous, I will say from the outset that I think we humans are already intrinsically loving like other mammals, just that we have forgotten because of our intense resentment, our vengeful feelings, our selfishness, our high competitiveness and other acquired characteristics that do not correspond to our fundamental nature but to our collective neurosis.

In this chapter I will develop specifically the point of view that if we want to come to be more loving toward our fellows, we must first learn to love ourselves and to do so, in turn, we must understand the extent to which we reject, disdain, push, and mistreat ourselves, without knowing it, of course, because of our generalized psychological blindness.

Also, before properly beginning to talk about what treating ourselves well would involve, I should explain something that Freud discovered in his time but which never came to be truly understood by our culture: that our very civilization is a sort of cage that robs our instinctive self of its freedom. However not even Freud himself came to understand that it was questionable whether the pathogenic civilization that we have had a desire to ensure that we be good rather than bad and only his heirs came to label Freud as a pessimist in his suspicious and implicitly criminalizing view of human nature.

Freud spoke of neurosis as a result of "the vicissitudes of instincts" in a social environment that stimulates the operation of a "reality principle " at the expense of the "pleasure principle" and later Herbert Marcuse explained at greater length the antagonism between civilization and Eros.

But what is that 'reality principle', according to which the expression of instincts should be inhibited despite their repression leading to their transformation into symptoms? Or, rather, what is that *reality* according to which the individual should understand that his pleasure should be, if not sacrificed, always relegated?

Although it is understandable that sometimes one can prefer to not eat at a specific time for reasons of health, or to save scarce foodstuffs for tomorrow, there is no doubt that, in general, the reality to which we must adapt ourselves is the reality of our participation in the civilized world, which leads, more exactly, to our socialization in a patriarchal world. In turn, we can understand this as a world made up of people whose inner life is ruled by a power resembling the paternal aspect (intellectual and normative) of our trifocal psyche.

Once we understand it in this way, it seems to us that Freudian language when speaking of reality (when reality is that of despotism) contains a subtle justificatory concealment; perhaps a diplomatic gesture by Freud, who was a person sufficiently adapted to his time so as not to have come to believe in the liberation of the instinctive nature nor in shaking off the condemnatory or vilifying patriarchal attitude of the inner animal (even at the end of his life).

Far from having reached the notion of the generosity of human nature (like the mystics of times past and the humanists of today), we know that even in his final thoughts Freud thought that people are potentially evil and dangerous (more specifically, cannibals and parricides), as a result of which it is not only convenient for us but in fact necessary to have the collective control of justice, jails, and the police, all considered unnecessary by the so-called primitives.

Following Freud, however, who after having intuited the morbid nature of repression did not dare to adopt a revolutionary attitude, D. H. Lawrence and Wilhelm Reich completed his thinking and in view of that, we can vindicate the pioneer who through his vast contributions to consciousness managed to set in motion a revolution in any event: one that has transformed us a great deal, no matter how much at this time the forces of power battle against it.

Let us now examine more closely the patriarchal oppression of the inner child (which is nothing other than our instinctive self or inner animal) and reflect on its consequences.

To begin with, let us go back to that period some six thousand years ago, as James DeMeo so convincingly explains in his book *Saharasia*, when the Earth was like a ball of ice with the exception of an area between the Sahara desert and the Ukraine, where agriculture was developed for the first time, after which the entire Earth underwent a progressive warming.

DeMeo suggests that after we became sedentary and developed a sort of culture that many today call matristic, we had to again become nomadic because the agricultural production of the earth no longer managed to sustain us. We can imagine the migrations that took place, because we have known analogous migrations in later periods of history until the beginning of the Middle Ages and it is easy to understand the toughening up of those who had to survive by killing; particularly in the cases of those whose voracity, exacerbated by need, came to turn on other human beings.

We are the descendants of those rapacious men who learned to survive through the exercise of force, power, insensitivity, and shrewdness. No matter how much we brag about our civilized condition. Only recently has it begun to be understood that we are nothing more than barbarians who have learned to self-idealize, covering up our barbarity by celebrating the greatness of our culture and likewise declaring "barbaric" those more primitive peoples who barely even hunted animals, let alone progressing as we did toward enslaving despotism and becoming warriors. Incidentally, before our ancestors, who were accustomed to hunting animals devoted themselves to hunting the goods of their fellow human beings or other human beings themselves, it is more than likely that they had learned to enslave women.

Taking possession of a woman by a strong male is a very old concept and perhaps marked the beginning of the history of slavery, as well as of systemic injustice. It would seem that men began to later extend this process of taking possession to other men, beginning with foreign tribes or rival peoples, and we can imagine that women's hearts shrank as they witnessed man's harshness toward man, powerless to act. Nonetheless, it is difficult not to realize that from the same beginning of this historic period those women must have seen themselves reduced to the powerless position of domestic slaves before the imperative triumph of aggression over tenderness.

We can imagine that perhaps it had been necessary for men to take power despite women's feelings in order to save our species, no matter how true it is that the wielding of this power became obsolete a long time ago. In any event, over time men's authority over women and children (necessary for war) became explicit in the institution of the *paterfamilias*, which established as law the dominion of the father over his wife and children. It is likely that this tyrannical figure of the father of the family was the result of agreement between men acting in collusion in the political realm, a mutual understanding, one could say, of taking political power and replicating this in the family setting.

If women had to be forced accomplices of the betrayal of solidarity that masculine violence implies, the children had to suffer this violence most directly, since they always have the greatest need for tenderness and are the most sensitive to violence.

Just as the subordination of women in patriarchal society is echoed in the relative eclipse of the feminine (especially tenderness, empathy and sense of community) in our minds, we can consider that the relegation, chronic frustration and impotence felt by children in the patriarchal world is reflected in the fact that the inner child within each of us has become like the living dead, forgotten even by itself.

What choice can a child have when faced with the punishing and threatening patriarchal power? Thus, a third part of our inner nature has remained in a state of latency, halted in its development and reduced to a condition comparable to that of being a prisoner. In addition, by turning against nature, the civilized world has not just wanted to control and exploit the external world but it has also controlled and exploited in a similar fashion the inner animal (or inner child) of each and every person, which has lead to us becoming a self-domesticated species.

This turn against our instinctive nature does not just impoverish us but also, by depriving ourselves of the organismic intelligence of our animal self, makes us in a certain way clumsy in how we lead our lives; we get sick: it makes us unhappy more than we realize and therefore greedy and vindictive.

Being healthy is a loving state in which love for one's fellow beings seems to gush in healthy people, from an overflowing fountain that is the love they feel for themselves.

In other words, to love others is natural in people who love themselves. However in our world, which has defined itself as Christian, the precept of "love thy neighbor as yourself" is neither practiced nor preached but instead, we exercise a compulsive altruism in which loving oneself is forbidden, since when children exhibit this they are called selfish and they are made to feel they are doing something bad.

Selfishness and love of oneself are fundamentally different and one could even say that selfishness is an attempt to fill the emptiness left behind by people's lack of true love for themselves.

How can people collectively love themselves if they are educated through demands and punishments to turn them into beasts of burden, which ultimately serve the production of the community? Even the mothers who most love their children foresee that to prevent their suffering they must make them into good beasts of burden in our implicitly oppressive society and therefore able to compete advantageously in the labor market.

I go back to the origins of our patriarchal society to observe that in times of hunger and migration, children, who had to adapt to a world at war and who must have suffered more than anyone due to deprivation, also had to learn to endure hardship.

DeMeo writes in this regard, and I will again cite a paragraph that already appears in *Healing Civilization*:

"Hunger and malnutrition are a severe trauma from which the survivors rarely escape unharmed. Many die, families are separated, and often, infants and children alike are abandoned, with the great suffering that all this entails. Malnutrition severely effects the emotions of surviving children, who try to disconnect themselves from the thirst and the overwhelming heat, they isolate themselves emotionally from the painful world, simultaneously suffering from a severe atrophying of the entire brain and nervous system due to a lack of protein and calories. Even when those malnourished children later receive the nourishment and water they need, they are deeply affected, emotionally and neurologically, in such a way that their behavior is forever altered. More specifically, an inhibition is implanted in them of all the impulses toward pleasure, their external nature, and a rejection of deeper forms of bodily pleasure, both in their expression of mother-child interaction as well as in gestures of affection between the sexes. Also, the vision that the child retains of the mother who did not know how to protect or feed it during the period of hunger, is tainted from that moment on with suspicion and hate. These attitudes and behaviors (of a deeply protoplastic nature) are transmitted to the next generations, independent of the climate, through the social institutions that reflect the character structure of the average individual in each era."[2]

These considerations help us to understand that civilization has not merely brought about an overvaluation of violence at the expense of tenderness but also an opposition to pleasure, that is to say, an ascetic spirit. From this comes that antagonism toward the body that has manifested itself so often in the history of religions.

In view of these considerations then, it is clear that if we want to achieve health in our emotional world and our relationships with our fellow humans, we must recover above all the love for our own instinctive nature; which would be the same as truly loving ourselves, in this way putting an end to our current criminalization of pleasure and inhibition of our spontaneity. Without this, collective happiness, the love of our fellow man or the development of the creative potential of our nature does not seem conceivable to me.

While much attention has been placed on how patriarchal culture has tried to shift the blame for its ills on to women (as for example in the figure of Eve), I think that the crimi-

[2] James DeMeo. Saharasia: *The 4000 BCE Origins of Child Abuse, Sex-Repression, Warfare and Social Violence, In the Deserts of the Old World.* Natural Energy Works, Oregon, 2011.

nalization of instinct has gone far deeper and by demonizing the holy serpent of the matristic cultures, not only has the animal been criminalized but also childish spontaneity.

No matter how much people have wanted to interpret original sin as curiosity (Kafka), as the arrogance of humans wanting to be like gods (Goethe) or as a desire for freedom, it seems to me that the story of Genesis hides (like the famous fig leaf and the shame of nakedness) a sexual component; a *temptation* that is symbolized in the eating of the forbidden fruit. This "Lord" conceived of by patriarchal man, who did not want men to eat from the Tree of Life and come to be like gods, must not have been a benign god (contrary to appearances).Because of this, modern people can sympathize with the gnostics, who considered this demiurge god of the Indo-Aryans and Semites a sort of demon. The fact that in our early history spiritual knowledge was transmitted through a patriarchal culture distorted it and the wisest of their time probably knew how to understand it, no matter how much the deadly laws attributed to the celestial tyrant made it dangerously blasphemous to say so.

I hope that no one thinks that my wish to show that the prohibition of the (reptilian) desire already appears in our foundational text is based on academic enthusiasm, rather I mean to suggest how profoundly revolutionary the passage from the patriarchal model to the holistic and heterarchic or triunitary model required by our individual and collective health would be. Nonetheless, the first step must be the necessary recovery of love for ourselves, that is to say, for our inner child.

It would seem that love of ourselves, already prescribed by the Christian precept, is something perfectly compatible with our culture but it is worth recognizing the trickery that this view entails. A trickery that ignores the Freudian truth of a deep-rooted taboo against the spontaneous expression of our desires and the anthropological truth of our exploiting and self-domesticating condition.

It is clear that in order to recover the capacity to love one's neighbors, which we so urgently need in order to emerge from our condition of collective violence, we must recover love for ourselves and the corresponding animal health that we have neglected while aspiring to supposedly higher things.

That love for ourselves which we need to recover should not be confused with a simple 'improvement of self-esteem', which educators are sometimes recommended to be aware of these days. Instead, this must be a true love. It will be one that translates into action, the relevant action in this case being putting an end to the violence against ourselves that we have ceased to even notice, to the degree that we discount the fact that our inner world is that of a duality of pursuer/pursued, accuser/accused, enslaver/slave.

The task of education, therefore, must in this case be similar to that of deep psychotherapy, which aims to guide people toward a transformation from an internalized police regime toward an organismic functioning. Except that the transformation of an adult is one thing and the prevention of the establishment of such an intra-psychic police regime in a child is quite another. The child will have been contaminated to a certain degree by the culture through upbringing but can be more easily returned to freedom than an adult whose personality has fully crystallized.

We could say that the key word for this process that leads learners toward being able to self-regulate is "freedom" (particularly in the sense of freeing ourselves from the traditional repressive yoke of patriarchal culture). Nonetheless when freedom is discussed, we must realize that to achieve fullness of life, not only spontaneity and creativity are important, but also the ability to place limits (which involves the ability to detach and renounce) and that these things are not incompatible with each other.

The ancient Greeks already seemed to have understood this thoroughly, since two complementary divinities presided over their mysteries, figures who were precisely related to the unlimited and limitation, the surrender to spontaneity and control: Dionysus and Apollo.

It could be said that in our culture we have lived a hegemony of control and we must recover spontaneity. It seems to me that it would be a creative task of education to look for the best way of teaching discipline without falling into a spirit of repression. To do this, as I have already suggested in other contexts, not just the experiences of pioneers such as the Wilds in the Pestalozzi school in Ecuador would be productive but also the precedents of shamanism and gestalt therapy, which are fields in which such a synthesis has already been made and therefore these are living examples that this is possible.

CHAPTER 5

Educating for Love Through Self-Awareness

EMOTIONAL EDUCATION is not the only measure that needs to be introduced into the current educational curriculum that is offered, because the critical times we are going through also require us to be wise. This does not simply mean knowing the things that science teaches but perhaps most importantly for the future of our violent and competitive society, as well as for our development as human beings, becoming more benevolent, empathetic, and caring.

I have already said that if we want to be more loving toward our neighbors, we must do so from the basis of a healthy love for ourselves and that we fool ourselves by thinking that love for ourselves is something that we can take for granted. On the contrary, love of people for themselves is something as lacking in the world today as is love for our neighbors.

If we fool ourselves in this regard it is because we confuse the healthy love of ourselves with selfishness, the latter of which is nothing more than a poor and problematic substitute of the former. It is also due to our tendency to be unaware of the degree of rejection we harbor with regard to ourselves, the little care with which we treat ourselves in our demands, and the degree to which we devalue ourselves, thus ignoring our capabilities and potentials.

We fool ourselves, as well, when we declare that we are in agreement with the Christian precept of love, which exhorts us to love our neighbors as we love ourselves. In reality we are a culture that does not practice what is preached and does not even notice this. Our cultural practice, far from encouraging children to develop a healthy love of themselves, prematurely demands of them an unmeasured altruism, interpreting as selfishness what is nothing other than the natural expression of their desires and thereby perpetuating, through their upbringing, that implicit, guilty self-rejection that we now see as being intrinsic to human nature.

I come now to the subject of developing our capacity of love for our fellow humans, which we can understand as the maternal aspect of our nature: benevolence, generosity, compassion and empathy or the ability to put ourselves in the place of others.

The fact that for some two millennia we have oriented ourselves according to the Christian idea of love without having managed to become loving people (instead, on the contrary, we have managed to create an increasingly more violent society) is something that we could interpret as an historic proof that for the development of love neither *the ideal of love,* nor sermons, nor good intentions are enough.

In order to attain the ideal of love we need a method, call it a teaching of love or a therapeutic process and I am convinced that we have the resources for this, even if the relevant know-how has not yet been integrated into our educational systems.

I have already explained one aspect of this know-how when stating that one of the foundations of loving ones neighbors is the decriminalization of desire and pleasure through the Dionysian spirit (which values happiness and gives back to people a trust in their natural impulses) I therefore now propose to consider other aspects, beginning with the recognition that something similar to *an exorcism of malevolence* is no less important for the cultivation of benevolence.

For this, it would be a good idea for educators to correct the prejudicial and already obsolete vision of human nature as implicitly destructive and to understand that generosity is intrinsic to a healthy mind, despite the fact that true mental health is more the exception than the rule, probably since that mythical "fall from paradise" of our species. That universal neurosis discovered by Freud prevails in the human condition to such a degree that what is considered *normal* deserves to instead be called (as Pierre Weil, founder of the University for Peace in Brasilia has rightly proposed) *normotic*.

In light of such example, to educate for love should above all be to educate for emotional health, a task that begins with the recognition of the sickness and that involves a coming together of the fields of education and public health.

Insofar as today the intervention of educational psychologists or psychotherapists only seems relevant in the case of exceptionally disturbed students, in the case of the others our educational culture has insisted on maintaining a clear distinction between its tasks and those of psychotherapy (despite it seeming that an increasing number of children reach school damaged by the precariousness of their family environments, as well as by the fact that their parents live growingly enslaved by an increasingly less-benevolent labor market, which only increases its demands). It seems to me that now is the moment for education to integrate the essential elements of therapeutic culture and to accept its responsibility with regard to the emotional development of learners.

This does not mean that education should adopt the language or forms of psychotherapy. It would be enough for educators to be educated with regard to recognizing emotional pathologies, as well as in the understanding that (as Buddha, Socrates, and Saint Augustine have already lucidly described) behind and beneath our ill will and our pernicious desires lies the lack of awareness of our inner life.

Today, the word 'neurosis' has fallen into disuse in reference to an emotional disturbance that underlies many pathologies of the personality and other clinical symptoms, rather (primarily through transpersonal psychology) the word 'ego' has entered into circulation in our culture, which has taken on a different meaning to that which it had been given in psychoanalysis. It is said that a person acts "from his ego" when he is acting from a relatively automatic zone of his psyche, characterized not just by a limitation of awareness but also by narcissism, egocentrism, and the prominence of neurotic needs.

We could say that the true self coexists within ourselves, along with a conditioned self that we have developed during childhood, as a defense against the conflict with a sick world.

This duality is usually alluded to as being between essence and personality, or alternatively, between a true self and the ego.

Using this language, we could say that love is part of our essence, which finds itself imprisoned by our personality or ego, in such a way that to recover our loving potential we must free our true self of the defensive childhood conditioning that is part of our personality. In alternative language, we could say that to reach love, we need to transcend the limits of our ego and its destructive emotions. But how?

In a word: through self-awareness. Knowing oneself is already a first step toward looking at oneself from the outside, which is dissociating ourselves from what we are looking at and as self-awareness transforms our relationship with our emotions, we can talk of a transformative self-awareness.

It turns out, therefore, that the path to love cannot be considered separately from the path to self-awareness, and that emotional education must include the understanding of that dark side of ourselves that we usually prefer not to recognize, and which blocks the expression of our loving potential.

The road to self-awareness is made up of different levels, of which the most basic is the first contact with our experiences, particularly with what we feel in each given moment.

Although we could define paying attention to our feelings in the moment as a discipline of self-observation, it is also part of what is usually called meditation, which today is being introduced into the medical field under the term *mindfulness*.

However, it is not enough to know what we feel from one moment to the next: we must be able to understand how our isolated observations are organized in patterns that influence our actions. Therefore, emotional self-observation should be complemented with the observation and understanding of our relationships with people and with the observation of how motivations that were unrecognized until now underlie the things we do and say.

The understanding of how we think is also an important part of self-awareness, which in turn involves the recognition of how many of our ways of seeing others and interpreting what happens to us are irrational and dysfunctional. All this can be summed up in *becoming aware of the cognitive nucleus of our ego*.

Also of great importance is understanding the story of our own life and especially how during the first stage of this we were affected by certain painful experiences that made us what we are now; since in response to our childhood suffering we have developed certain fixed behavioral patterns that have become obsolete or which interfere with our having a creative response to our current situation.

Finally, it is particularly important for us to understand how such behavior patterns articulate in our specific personalities and how our personalities are characterized by the predominance of one or another of a series of destructive emotions.

As for understanding the personality itself, in my view the most useful resource is the application of a body of knowledge that is usually referred to as the Enneagram. The application of the Enneagram to the personality, which seems to have been transmitted in the past as a secret knowledge of an esoteric Christian school of central Asia, has filtered into popular culture in our present, so that there are innumerable courses on it and many books have been published, all of which indicates the impact of such information on the public.

I am not sure that it would be a good idea to teach children to recognize the psychopathology of their character, because this, which is still in development, is a response to an environment that they cannot control and it would be arrogant of current educational institutions to claim to offer their students a healthier or more healing environment.

I am convinced, however, that knowledge of the psychology of enneatypes, especially when presented in an experiential and not merely theoretical format, is a very important contribution to the training of educators and psychotherapists, therefore I include in this book (as a way of complementing this chapter on self-awareness) a more detailed explanation of that specific discipline.

I now return to the subject of transcending the ego, which is nothing other than a way of speaking about the need to heal within ourselves something like a parasitic mind, or an emotional plague that interferes and competes with the exercise of our loving vocation.

I have spoken of self-awareness as an important resource for this, however, therapeutic experience informs us that it is important to posses an understanding not only of what happens in our mind, but also of the living contact we have with our emotions. In turn, emotional expression is necessary for one to transcend the ego.

Little by little, over the history of psychoanalysis, the importance of the expression of childhood pain and rage has been recognized. With the arrival of humanistic psychology, catharsis and abreaction reached their peak through which an awareness of emotions repressed since childhood and inclusive access to forgotten memories is achieved. Therefore, concerning the understanding and re-elaboration of psychic digestion particular to childhood, it turns out that memory and understanding of what has happened to us are very linked with the expression of suffering and rage, which have usually been forgotten and repressed. It is particularly in our interests to understand childhood, since the attitudes adopted against pain from that period are the ones that limit the expression of our potential to love during adult life. More precisely, the behavioral patterns adopted in relation to our parents repeat in our adult life with the many people we have relationships with, whether in our love life or in our work relationships, which involve roles of authority.

Therefore, we must understand and heal those childhood patterns of parental relationship and thereby recover loving health, thus putting an end to such patterns if we want to see ourselves freed from the shadow of unresolved past situations in our current relationships.

How can we heal the triangle of our childhood relationship with our mother and father? Although almost all schools of psychotherapy have sought to achieve this, I do not know any method as noted for its efficiency and brevity as one that does not appear in textbooks or in the repertoire of the methods known to the academic world. Since nothing seems to me to be more relevant for the training of educators than for them to some day, having recovered their loving health, be able to sow love among their pupils, in the next chapter I will recount how I discovered this method, how I developed it, and how I have been applying it with considerable success over many years as part of the curriculum of the Seekers After Truth Program that I created some forty years ago and which is still being applied today in the training of educators and therapists.

Thus far, I have dealt with the necessary foundation of loving oneself in order to love one's neighbors as well as the need to purify the mind of the neurotic destructiveness that competes with love. Nonetheless, I have not yet tackled the more specific subject of the *cultivation* of love and in so doing, I want to share my theoretical vision in this regard, which I usually refer to as my theory of the three loves.

Briefly, this approach acknowledges three basic dimensions in the experience of love. Just as the practically infinite chromatic spectrum can be understood as the combination of three basic colors and in effect it is perceived by three different color receptors in the retina and just as the infinite multiplicity of points in space can be described in three basic dimensions (length, width and height), this is also true with love. Even though we cannot describe it, define it in words, or enclose it in concepts, certain of its fundamental aspects can indeed be defined as its dimensions: Eros or instinctive love, agape or compassionate love and the form of love that Socrates and Aristotle called filial, because of its close ties with friendship.

We could say that the compassionate or empathetic love, usually referred to as the love of one's neighbors, is an extension of maternal love beyond the immediate family. We could say that the love that comes into play in friendship is an appreciative love, which places more importance on values than on people and which is closely related in our experience to the early relationship of a boy or girl with his or her father. In the same way, we could relate compassion and empathy to maternal love and also to our mammalian, relational brain. By way of analogy, we could relate appreciative love (like the ideals themselves) to the figure of the father and to the intellectual function of the neocortex; we could also relate the instinctive love or Eros to our primitive or reptilian brain, which is not just like an *inner animal* but also like an *inner child*, in such a way that it establishes a correspondence between inner brains and personas.

We can also establish an equivalence between the three aspects of love and the three prescriptions contained in the Christian precept of "love thy neighbor as thyself and God above all things." For if the love of one's neighbor is empathetic, caring and maternal, love of the divine, which we usually call 'devotion', is a form of love of the father, even if devotion does not necessarily depend on a theistic philosophy and can also be called love of Dharma, or of the Tao, of the realization of one's potential, or even a love of justice, truth and other values.

It is the love of oneself that in this triple precept can be related to Eros, since it differs in quality from empathetic love by revolving around our inner child and its aspiration to happiness.

A corollary of the understanding that love is not a simple psychic energy but instead manifests in three different forms, is that it can at times reveal itself in a qualitatively incomplete form, in the sense that the person can be intensely erotic but lack compassion, or be highly compassionate without being able to feel much appreciation, or be able to admire while lacking in empathy or enjoyment. There is then a crippled love, in contrast to a good love in which the qualities of love are in harmony. If the three loves are the expression of our three brains or inner personas, it could therefore be expected that since we aspire to an intra-psychic integration that will make us effectively three-brained beings, as Gurdjieff proposes, we must also aspire to achieving a balance between our ways of loving.

I have written this thought in such a way that perhaps it seems a mere theoretical hypothesis but over years of observation and educational experimentation, I can add that I have come to consider it an undeniable fact that people, according to their nature, manifest certain abilities alongside certain disabilities with regard to love. According to the enneatypes, people suffer from specific difficulties and overcoming them will require specific correction in the area of the development of love. Schizoid personalities, for example, are defined by the underdevelopment of empathy and for them more than anyone, the development of compassion will be important. In histrionic personalities, admiring love is underdeveloped and in those who are fearful and mistrusting, it is erotic love which is lacking. In view of such situations, I believe it is important for education to adopt the idea of a program of emotional education that keeps in mind the different forms of love and the impoverishment of our inner life than can result from the tendency toward a unilateral development. I think that my presentation of this subject is sufficient for now and I propose to continue developing it later, in connection with my own method of personal and professional development for therapists and educators, again, known as the SAT Program.

CHAPTER 6

Wisdom Beyond Ego:

CULTIVATING AWARENESS WITH ENNEAGRAM

D**URING THE PAST DECADES**, the great interest awoken by the Enneagram through its applications to the study of personality have spread from Chile to China, to the point where a "Day of the Enneagram" has been established in the calendar, and businessmen interested in the subject began to attend courses from Amsterdam and Norway, to Korea and Indonesia.[3] This interest lies in the stimulus that a personality map and a corresponding view of neurosis has represented for self-awareness, because of which, beyond what I have said until now about the various aspects of self-awareness, I will also include this theoretical formulation that has been of such use in the training of therapists as well as educators and more recently, some who work in the business world. To do so, I will reproduce a talk about the

[3] World Enneagram Day has been instituted by the International Enneagram Association.

psychology of enneatypes given in 2011 in the Aula Magna of the School of Law at the University of Buenos Aires.

A Contribution of the Psychology of Enneatypes to an Integral Model of Health:

Thank you for the warm welcome. I have been asked to talk to you about how the Enneagram can benefit integral health, and I do not know if an "integral health service" exists, which by definition must be one that does not only concern itself with physical complaints but also the emotional aspect of illnesses. It seems to me that one does not. Today, the use of psychotherapy in medical institutions is in decline. According to what practicing friends tell me, they must attend some five or six people per hour and the only thing they can do is give them drugs. Moreover, in a world that is impoverishing itself to such a degree that psychotherapy costs too much time and money (and those who have money do not have time), not only are resources become scarce, but also hours. Furthermore, psychotherapy requires a spirit of searching, a self-questioning and it seems that this also is becoming scarce with progress and modernity.

We are not just in a more secular society but also an increasingly more scientific one, where humanist disciplines are becoming a sort of superstition in the view of the majorities. That is why I propose that psychotherapy must find its place in education; that education should be for human development, that instead of serving to reproduce that which is wrong in the world from generation to generation, it should perpetuate the so-called values, which in reality are half values and half plagues. However, it is not for human development; if it tried to be for human development and not the creation of robots, it would need to take many tools from psychotherapy and spiritual traditions, and I do not know if it will manage to do so.

Lidia Grammatico said that the SAT Program is experiencing great success and it is true that it is indeed doing so among educators but not in the world of government, nor in the bureaucratic world that rules what is done in education, not among the ministers of education. I suspect that education is doing perfectly well what it sets out to do, which is to educate for production and not for human development, to educate for the perpetuation of a system of social utilization; there are those who fear greatly that people will begin to think another way and even fear that Socratic call, beckoning them to know themselves. There is not much in education about knowing oneself, which sometimes is confused

with studying psychology, when these are two completely
different things.

But I digress: rather, I have been asked to talk about the
Enneagram. There is a great movement in the world around
the Enneagram: there are many badly-named courses given
on the Enneagram which, if the people who taught them
knew, should be called courses aiding in the understanding
of the Enneagram or in the application of the Enneagram; I
have called it the Psychology of Enneatypes.

The person who spoke of the Enneagram for the first
time in the West did not present it as something relating
to personality but instead related to certain Gnostic laws.
This person was Gurdjieff and he used the Enneagram as
the conjunction of the Law of Three and the Law of Seven.
What was meant by the Law of Three? It is something similar to what Hegel said: in every phenomenon, there is a
polarity, a Yin and a Yang, a negative force and a positive
one and in addition, a synthesis factor, reconciling: to
understand things one must take this perspective, this third
element of synthesis.

The Law of Seven is more difficult: it refers to certain characteristics of cycles. For example, we have a week ordered
in seven days; where did they come from? The Egyptians

already had them; they were in all cultures, each of them dedicated to a different god. I do not know if the students of cyclical phenomena would have formulated something similar today to this idea that cycles have seven stages. I was a disciple of a Polish philosopher who said that there was a dialectic of five stages in the history of western thought: this approached to a point the Law of Seven.

I recount all this only to give a point of reference, since Gurdjieff, the first who mentioned the Enneagram, talks of very different things from those who have popularized this symbol. The Enneagram has become quite famous for its application to the personality, but it could seem to refer to a pretentious discipline, an academic branch of knowledge that will interest some but not others, because why would we be interested in personality?

Perhaps it would be more realistic to say that this knowledge that has been so enthusiastically spread recently is a *theory of evil*, a theory of why we suffer, a theory of why the world has problems. That is why it is vital; it is not as specialized as it might seem. Going back to what has been said about the origin of suffering, I prefer to speak of evil: it is a far tougher word. The measure of humanity's uneasiness is related to the spread of evil and ethical decay. Perhaps the first to formulate a great theory of evil was Buddha, who told us that suffering is explained through desire. Schopenhauer wanted to import Buddhism into his philosophy and placed the emphasis on the man who suffers because he wants too much. In reality, the word *tanha*, which is used in the Buddhist context, does not mean "desire" exactly, rather it is something like a hyper desire, a pathological desire; I think that the closest thing in our world is that which in psychoanalysis is called *orality*: remaining fixated on what was lacking in our childhood and becoming excessively leech-like. We all want more, we all want that which we are missing, all of us are missing a bit of mothering, because our mothers inherited the same vices as all human beings, as our civilization involves the transfer of a plague through the generations, just as said in Judaism. In reality, what Buddha said so explicitly, is also said in the myth of the fall of humankind, of the expulsion from the original paradise, a legend that is not just Jewish, but which is also told by the Greeks, the ancient Mexicans, and many other cultures.

The idea that we constantly progress, the social applications of the theory of Darwin, the evolution of society as an echo of the notion of the evolution of the species, is a new idea. Before Darwin, the general vision was that the world was getting increasingly worse. In some ancient cultures, there was a historic vision of a Golden Age, from which we supposedly passed to a Silver Age (the matristic age, we could say today) which was not a matriarchy, since it was not a society of women who gave orders (giving orders is a thing of patriarchy, of masculine dominion), but rather a society that revolved around the values of life, fertility, the community, and the environment, different from later warrior values. At some given moment we became warriors, in a period that the Greeks called the Bronze Age or the Age of Heroes, and then we moved into a deteriorated warrior age.

In Dante's *The Divine Comedy* there is a great symbol, the Ancient of Crete, who has a golden head, a silver chest, a belly of bronze, and legs of iron, except for his right foot, which is clay. I like this figure very much as the symbol of patriarchy, which is progressively deteriorating, which was originally a warrior patriarchy, that after the period of weapons, armies, and explicit power, has transformed into a period of commercial power: this commercial power more resembles clay than iron; it would seem that clay would be less violent than iron but it is not a lesser power, as we know. In this period, it would seem that at last we have managed to turn this idea of the open society Popper talked about: a society without tyrants into reality. "The tyrants are falling, we're leaving them behind," some say. There have always been bosses and underlings in the world, oppressors and the oppressed, but now we are in a strange society where there are only the oppressed; there are no oppressors What oppresses us now are the laws of the marketplace and no one controls them. The issue is that there are people who prefer to be the ones who give the orders.

By now, you will have realized that I have a certain tendency to go off on tangents. What I am telling you does not have much to do with the application of the Enneagram to personality, except for what I said about the existence of excessive desires and excessive aversions; we want certain things too much and behind that there is an invisible factor, a more powerful factor, which Buddha called ignorance. That theory of Buddha, that ignorance is the cause of all evil, was repeated by Socrates and was again repeated in the attempts of the Fathers of Church to explain Original Sin. One of the factors for discerning Original Sin is ignorance, a word that is not very well understood in our modern world without many explanations, because we are in a world with little wisdom and the world of knowledge does not recognize this phenomenon of ignorance, that has nothing to do with a lack of education. That is why perhaps the best term is the one used by José Saramago in his book *Blindness*: when one talks of blindness one means specifically that interference with the understanding of things, which is like not seeing even though one has all the data in view.

Therefore, the Enneagram is a geometric figure having a triangle for its center, and in that triangle one can discern three factors that, in Buddhism, are called the three poisons and are represented as three animals that attack one another and form a vicious circle. They are ignorance, desire, and aversion. In the upper part, we have the factor of ignorance: the inability to see. On the right side is the excess of desires, and in the left angle is the aversion factor. It was difficult for me to come to the conviction that the three poisons were the same as the structure of the Enneagram. What gave me the key was encountering experts in the typology of early Buddhism. I am a gentle person, easygoing, I never wanted to hurt anyone, but from the Buddhist typology I am an aversive type, which means to live in a sort of retreat, or being a misanthrope. Before beginning to become interested in transformation, I was a withdrawn and contemptuous person, with adults since I was a child and as an adult, with the world in general. However, there are other forms of aversion in the Enneagram: that which corresponds to Gluttony, which corresponds to the capital sin of the same name in the Christian tradition and does not sound like an aversion but instead someone who has an appetite, who thinks too much of pleasure. From the point of view of ancient Buddhist typology however, we would say that a person with a sweet tooth is a masked criminal: someone in the role of the fox of the fables, who harbors much rebellion but never shows it directly.

The Enneagram is an application that involves a typology, an awareness of human types. These are not just recognized through the typologies of the enneatypes: anyone who likes literature could find them in the novels of all periods. In reality, there are not that many, since novels have not existed for very long but a considerable number of them consist of character constructions. In the theater, one could illustrate a large part of these exclusively with Shakespeare. So, why is the Enneagram so famous?

In the modern world, many types are also recognized. There is the DSM, of universal use, where the types called histrionic, schizoid, avoidant and so many others are described. They are the same types that the description of the Enneagram recognizes. So, why has the Enneagram become so popular instead of the DSM? Because the DSM is very boring. It is used because there is no other choice: if you are a psychotherapist, you need to deal with insurance companies and formulate a diagnosis so that the insurance will cover it, so suddenly we had these definitions. When I studied psychiatry, I received vague descriptions of these personalities and over the years, I have seen how they have been refined by pressures of the economic system. In psychiatry, it is necessary to have a precise diagnosis although they are of little interest in the first place because if one wants to enclose oneself in the diagnoses of the DSM V (the latest revision), one immediately begins to realize that they concern extreme cases of pathology. Quickly, one can see that they are not antisocial, nor sadistic, nor borderline, nor schizoid, nor even histrionic as described in the treatise, since all of them suffer much more spectacular symptoms than those one recognizes in oneself. So, it is not a system that clearly applies to each person, it is not a system of coordinates where everyone can find themselves and see with more clarity than they saw before positioning themselves on the map. There is the question: it is not a system that applies to everyone and that sheds light. The Enneagram, on the other hand, is an application that casts the light that both the DSM and the European Diagnostic Manual fail to provide. The Enneagram is not merely descriptive: it does not just say that the schizoid has this, that and the other character traits but instead formulates a psychology of enneatypes; that is what I will call them from now on. This psychology expresses that there is not just one nature but instead it has two focuses: in the first place, an emotional focus, a basic neurotic need, an exaggerated feeling that permeates that form of character, equivalent to the famous cardinal sin, which in the schizoid corresponds to avarice, for example. In classic iconography, avarice is represented as in Bosch's famous work exhibited in the Prado Museum: a solitary person in the darkness hoarding his gold; it is a solitary man who is replacing the world with what he has in his pockets, who accumulates resources within himself in order to not go toward the other. It is a nature that tends toward dehumanization, such as the famous King Midas, who wanted everything he touched to become gold, but who had not considered that he could touch a person and without realizing it touched his beloved daughter and turned her into a golden statue. Thus, there are people who want to turn everything into gold but gold does not satisfy as much as humanity, although there is this pathology in which one wants to be more than human: in some people it takes the form of gold, whereas for others it tends toward the gold of the philosophers, a super value, a distillation of values. One who goes down this path realizes at that moment that both love and happiness can only be found in having contact with simpler people and not in finding monuments or paying homage to superhuman people.

Let us see how I can return from going off on this tangent. I said that what the application of the Enneagram to the personality offers is an understanding of characters that is much more interesting that other formulations. The way in which these characters are distributed on the map of the Enneagram allows for each one of them to be better understood in their context. This map consists of a triangle within a circle, and beyond that triangle, the circle is divided into nine points. These points are connected in a very particular way: one is connected with four below and from four there is a connection to two, which is on the right, before three; from two there is a connection to eight, above, etc.

We are not going to get into the whys and wherefores of those connections but it is a fascinating subject: when one sees something in a context, one begins to understand things in such a way that the neighboring connections illuminate the point that one wants to understand better. For example, why did the seven deadly sins become so famous? Sins had gone out of use some decades ago, they had become anti-quated, an item out of the catechisms; it cannot be said that there were people passionate about understanding the deadly sins. Once, the deadly sins were part of culture. When Dante wrote *The Divine Comedy* and placed the proud in a specific purgatory and the envious in another, there was a culture in which people recognized themselves, in which they knew that this or that sin was predominant in themselves; there was the idea that some people were primarily proud, others envious, etc. Why did they know the sins so well? Because the religious culture was very much alive and because the great specialists in this subject, those who best formulated this doctrine, the Desert Fathers, were still recognized as great authorities for the Christian world.

For a long time, the doctrine about the deadly sins was an unwritten knowledge. The first to write on the subject was a monk of the 4th century, Evagrius Ponticus, who called the sins errors. In that time, the idea that the sins were errors already existed, although the word "sin" already alluded to a projectile that missed the mark: a ballistic term, today we would speak of deviations of psychic energy. It seems that the description of these sins was not Christian in origin: there is no reference to them in the Gospels and I encountered a perfect enumeration of the sins and their antidotes in an ode by Horace, more or less contemporary to Christ. Thus, while the idea of sin had not yet appeared in Christianity, classical culture was already aware of them. How did the Greeks know of this doctrine? It seems that there was a Hellenic esoterism, the roots of which had Babylonian origins. At least, that is what I was told by the person who showed me: Oscar Ichazo.

Now, thanks to the Enneagram, the sins have once again become current, when they had since become something so boring. The problem with the sins is that religious tradition has considered them as if they were crimes: ecclesiastical authoritarianism criminalized sin. It is much more interesting to correct our failings in the moment we identify them. It is hard to understand that the sins are obstacles for our own life when they are presented as violations of a Divine Law; if one lives so that God does not get angry up in heaven, one forgets one's own interests. In yoga one does not say: "don't do this, don't do that," as happens in the Biblical commandments. Rather, in yoga, it is as if there were an implicit commandment to not command: before meditating, it is said that people should control their mind, and to do that people should be capable of not lying, of not doing harm.

I remember a joke in which different national styles competed in a contest of proposals asking people not to smoke in buses. The German says: "Smoking is forbidden." While the American says: "Please, don't smoke." And the Jew says: "What do you *earn* by smoking?" Yoga is like that, a little more strategic and it asks you: "What do you get out of going along there when it is better to go along here?" It does not use the language of authoritarian command. I think that a factor that has encouraged people to be more interested in the Enneagram is that it has presented itself in a context of self-awareness in which one understands that those sins are not violations of divine mandates. It is difficult for people to be happy or to reach a state of higher consciousness if they are very ambitious, if they are focused on their own image. So, when people begin to understand first-hand the meaning of those sins, they become a vital issue and people begin to understand that the sins are like mental parasites to which one is offering one's energy. These outside forces that have taken possession of the mind itself roost in those who protect themselves too much from themselves, until they realize that all that anxiety for protection is just childhood conditioning that stems from a lack of mothering, from the emotional coldness that they felt as a child. Then they had the idea that the solution in life is to feel that warmth they were missing and in searching for it many things are lost, like the possibility of being stronger, losing courage, wandering like a vagabond through life.

The current context of interest in self-awareness created a new movement that originated with Gurdjieff, who on speaking of the Enneagram referred to stages in the process of evolution in a very abstract way. Many of us sought the origins of this knowledge. I formed part of the Gurdjieff school and those of us who were there were very intrigued: we did not understand Gurdjieff's life, we did not understand something that seemed to be half-baked. How many of you here have heard about Gurdjieff? I would like you to raise your hands. Approximately half. For those who have not had that contact, I would say that Gurdjieff was someone extraordinary in his time, a person unlike any other, one who impressed as a teacher not by taking on or adopting any role. He never portrayed himself as the representative of anything; instead it was a mystery from where he got that authority. He did not bring degrees with him like those psychologists who place on their office walls those bits of paper with the name of the university where they were qualified. Gurdjieff appeared a little before the Russian Revolution with a very large natural authority. He did not seem to want to be followed. Many have observed that when he taught, he did so through conversations in very noisy cafés where it was very difficult to hear him: it seemed as if he were placing a barrier before people so that they had to make an effort to learn. Over time, it became known that he had many influences, that he was a great synthesizer. One of his principal influences was that of Christian esoterism, but little more could be said about them because almost nothing is known about this. Some of us were searching for that mysterious source, hoping that there would be some contact. A factor for that hope was that Gurdjieff had first of all written an article titled "Herald of a Good Time That Will Come," in which he gave the idea that there is a mysterious school that is behind history and said that this would show itself in the world that was to come, that was yet to appear. Some were mistaken, like the famous and great searcher J. G. Bennet, when the Subud movement appeared and he took it to England thinking that it was what was foretold in Gurdjieff's prophecy. Subud is a discipline of spontaneous application: it seemed a perfect complement to the teachings of Gurdjieff, who was a master of conscious overexertion. Later it was seen that this was not the path. Some time ago I was in London, where I was invited to speak in the school of Ouspensky, who was a disciple of Gurdjieff: there, I saw that the original teachings had developed into different styles, related with Sufism and other schools.

In the search for a more direct contact with Gurdjieff's teachings, I found a book by Idries Shah, The Sufis. The author seemed to have had contact with that source and through it had evidence of the existence of a school that cultivated the method of speed. Later I came to know that Ichazo was in possession of that method. I became interested in Ichazo for various reasons but truth to tell, the most important of those was perfectly irrational. In 1969, I found myself in Miami, giving a weekend on Gestalt at the university. After finishing the workshop, I asked a few people in the group what they would recommend to me in Miami, because only at that moment had I realized that my next commitment was a week away, in Chicago. What was I to do in those days? To remain seemed a good idea and although I had left the decision to the last moment, I told myself that what I wanted to do was to write and there was an ideal climate there. So I asked various people from the group and they agreed that I should stay at the McAllister hotel. So, I checked in, called my home in Berkely and my wife told me: "There is a telegram for you from some Oscar Ichazo. Do you want me to read it to you?" I had never had any communication with Oscar Ichazo. I had known of him, but we had not exchanged a single word. I asked my wife to read the telegram to me and it said: "Get in touch with Jenny Pereda, at the Hotel McAllister, in Miami, on Thursday." It was Wednesday. The next day, I asked if she was in the hotel, but she had not arrived. I then went into the neighborhood for breakfast and then returned slowly window-shopping. I reached the hotel and I had an idea for the book I was writing, *The Divine Child and the Hero*, so I began to write. Around midday, I said to myself: "I am going to call down and ask if Jenny Pereda has arrived." At that moment, I picked up the phone and immediately found myself talking with Jenny Pereda, who was calling me. Then, I did not need to think about it any further: I took it as a sign. Many things like that have happened to me with Ichazo and that is why I put up with him, since he seemed to be rather unbearable. I came ready and desiring to find a true master: I once had as a master the great Fritz Perls and I told myself: "I will accept as a guide someone that I know through intuition is the right person for me, not for this reason or that but it has to be something more direct." I never felt anything like that with Ichazo, I never told myself: "This is my master, I want to work with him, I can surrender myself to him."

When I met with Ichazo in Chile, he told me, surprisingly, "My time is yours." I replied, "I don't plan to advertise for you." He answered me, "I know that this work will reach many people through you, so I have the responsibility to teach you very well; you can ask me anything you wish and I will pass on to you what I can." I spent three intense months with him and then I asked him: "Can I be your disciple, given the fact that I see you as a liar and a manipulator?" He smiled and told me, "Honor your suspicion, because you have been tricked in the past, but you will see: our path is very scientific, it doesn't need great veneration. The only thing needed is for you to work and let me work." Finally, he told me, "You are going to know the answer to your questions about the fruits of the work, but you will see the fruits of the work very soon, because I am going to make a very special proposition to you; this is a secret between us, but I am going to send you on retreat in the desert." He then spoke of how the following year he was going to send me to the Atacama Desert for forty days and that in that time I would find what I had been looking for my entire life. When I asked, "Can someone promise illumination?" He replied, "Sometimes, some people can" and I decided that despite all the mistrust I felt, it was worth giving myself to him for a time, as a working hypothesis. "I should take advantage of this," I thought. I had a profound spiritual experience; it was the beginning of my spiritual life.

I had searched for many years, I was a disciple of Suzuki, I practiced Zen meditation, but I still had not poked my head out of the clouds. So, I had what in Christianity is called an illuminative experience, which is not the end of the road but the true beginning. Ichazo, knowing that the Dark Night of the Soul would come, said to me, "All this is just a loan, you're going to lose it, you'll have to earn it for yourself." That is how it was. For a long time, I lived a spiritual awakening, a rebirth, a birth into another level of existence, which meant having an inner guide. For someone who goes through this, what interest does the Enneagram have? Why does learning about types of humans interest them? Ichazo had told me the year before, "I am going to give you my specialty." After that desert retreat, a little out of curiosity, I asked him, "What is it you're going to pass on to me, your specialty of the Enneagram?" "Yes, that's it," he answered me. "But we haven't had met up for some time and my stay here, in Arica, is coming to an end." "Don't worry," he replied, "I'll give you the keys." From one day to the next I began to recognize the natures of the people I met in the street. Now I cannot do that, but I had a very high capacity of recognition, just as one recognizes styles of painting or music. From there this entire psychology of the enneatypes emerged, this application of the Enneagram that has become so famous. For Ichazo never said, "Type one is like this, type three is like that," he did not even call them type one or type another but instead used insulting and ugly names. He called enneatype four "Ego Melan" ("Melancholy ego"), type five "Ego Stinge" (for avarice), etc. I baptized them in a rather more neutral way and that is what has been passed on.

In 1971, I began to work with a group in Berkeley in which I included descriptions of the types of ego and all those who began to teach the Enneagram in the United States were people to whom teachings from this initial group in Berkeley had trickled down. Making the descriptions teachable made it possible to diagnose with them. Before, character diagnosis was a standard practice that Ichazo did with us and we never knew how he did it, how he recognized that someone was a one or a four. There was no list of traits, there were no characteristics. Then, based on my courses, a phenomenon of great excitement in the people who began to learn with me took place, and many of them did not know how to remain quiet. All those who formed part of my group signed a written agreement that required them to keep this knowledge for their own use, without sharing it but very few of them could resist. Ichazo spoke of the temptation of directing or being the master: when one has a powerful instrument, one feels powerful and relies on it. The same thing happens with those who organize sessions with psychedelics: there is a power in knowing that you are giving an intense experience to another, although there are people who are not very good at doing it. Thus, a vulgarization of the Enneagram took place in North America, a very commercial vulgarization. I wanted to erase myself from the map. Sometimes I appear in a footnote as the one who passed on this information but in general, I do not even appear in the bibliography about the Enneagram. There are one or two references out there to the fact that it was I who introduced this knowledge into our culture but primarily it is known that I was part of that famous group in Arica and it is not imagined that I was someone who received from Ichazo a very special passing on of knowledge.

At the end of last year, I was invited to open the annual conference of the International Enneagram Association in Fortaleza, Brazil, where I heard that the Enneagram is reaching China. It seems that there is an interest in the Enneagram in practically every continent and my subject was that of the origins of the knowledge that is passed on in what are called "Enneagram courses." Making public my explanations lead to my later being invited to an event in Germany, to which people came from China, Indonesia, African countries, the Middle East, etc. It would seem that I owe this audience to the people who have pirated me. That saying "The devil doesn't know who he works for" is probably true.

As I said, a great interest in the Enneagram has been generated but about an Enneagram that is a little like the duck soup they talk of in Nasrudín's joke. I do not know if you know Mulá Nasrudín. He appears in different cultures. In Chile, for example, he is known as Don Otto and he is given Germanic characteristics. In the joke I want to tell you, Nasrudín, or Don Otto, is looking for the key to his house under the lighting in a plaza, and his friend comes and says to him, "Shall I help you?" They search and search and after a while the friend asks him, "Are you sure you lost it here?" Nasrudín answers, "No, I lost it at home, but the light here is better." No, that was not the joke I wanted, rather the one about the duck soup. This must be a sign of senility. So: someone gives Nasrudín a duck, his wife sticks it in a pot and makes a soup. The next day someone shows up and says he is a friend of the person who previously brought the duck and Nasrudín tells his wife, "See if you can add a little more water to what's left of the soup." So that is what they did. I like to tell the joke with many episodes, in which first the friend of the friend shows up, then the friend of the friend of the friend, then the friend of the friend of the friend of the friend. In any case, there comes a moment when the visitor is served a cup of totally transparent liquid and asks, "What is this, because it doesn't smell like anything" and the answer they give him is that it is "The soup of the soup of the soup of the soup of the soup of the friend of the friend of the friend. . ." This same degradation happens in the world of spirituality: it seems that the same information is handed on, but it loses its resolution just like photographs, when they are enlarged to a certain degree, they lose their detail, they do not have the same density. So, there is also the self-awareness of the self-awareness of the self-awareness etc. Sometimes, what is called self-awareness is nothing more than putting a label on the bottle that says: "Vintage of '32." Knowing that one is an enneatype two or an enneatype five should be an invitation to try the flavor of the liquid inside the bottle, but many people remain with the process of labeling the self-diagnosis and that which we call understanding is not that simple. To understand is an interconnection of one thing with another, of how everything is interconnected in life itself and of how certain inner things connect with specific episodes that one reads, that one lives. It is a process that takes time.

During the time that we were with Ichazo in Arica, we spent some three hours with him every day. One day, I calculated that, in total, he spent six hours teaching us about the Enneagram. His program was much broader, and had pretensions of being a program that he had called the Fourth Path, with physical and devotional elements that offered a mental panorama, a way of understanding, exercises of attention, exercises in presence etc. I tried to do the same with my own repertoire, although it is mistakenly said that the SAT Program is a process of awareness guided by the Enneagram. That is not completely correct, because in the program I try to teach the three areas of Buddhist meditation, which is no small thing. I bring collaborators who are skilled in Gestalt, who are skilled in theatrical work, etc. An important part of the SAT is Spontaneous Movement, a practice of surrendering oneself. There are many other elements: a process of catharsis of childhood pain and rage, this is oriented toward forgiving the parents so that, through the recognition of the loving ties to them, figures in our love life can be healed, such as for example the contact we have with people in authority, which are echoes of our own father. There are many elements in the SAT. I think that it is somewhat perverse to only use this information about the Enneagram.

Nonetheless, I should concentrate on the Enneagram. We begin with the well-known mortal, cardinal, or capital sins. Capital comes from the Latin *caput*, that is to say, the head. Ironically, the Vatican has lost interest in the classic capital sins, and it seems to me that this is because they do not understand them. When it is said, for example, that one of the sins of our time is the deterioration of the environment, something of great importance is being talked about. When it is said that another great sin in our modern humanity is the injustice in the distribution of riches, undoubtedly one of the greatest evils of the world is being talked about. However, that is not what is meant by Capital Sin, *caput*, which refers to the root sins, ways of being from which other consequences derive, that are behind our damaging actions. In fact, not just our damaging actions, because in the Christian capital sins there is an aspect of damaging outwards or toward oneself and also there is talk of a disturbance of the relationship with God. The sins draw us away from the divine, they are like false objectives, when the objective should be the Polar star: instead of guiding ourselves by it as we sail, we go off course. The corporate mentality leads the world today, not just in business but also in governments, in the economy, in the family and even in education, where the priority is money; the ancients would say that this corporate mentality is a sin that consists of placing money where God should be. The yearning for money is something like a drug addiction, something that hooks you too much, when you should have your attention placed on the highest purpose in life; that being a searching that is deeper than the search for utilitarian satisfactions.

So, the ancient notion of sin was very ambitious and the better one knows this repertoire of notions, the more one realizes how spot on they are. In practice, the sins have been rediscovered by psychotherapy. Only instead of there being seven of them, there are nine when applied to the Enneagram that has nine points. In the left angle is Fear, let us say cowardice. Why does Christianity not tell us that there is a sin of cowardice? Because, since the ecclesiastical system is authoritarian and hierarchical, it cannot preach courage or independence; the Church is too political to tell people to be brave and not surrender. We are in a hierarchal society in which those who are above know very well how to cultivate our obedience but all the psychoanalysis, the post-Freudian world, is a world in which it is patently obvious that behind our problems is fear. Already, since the early Freudian years of *Inhibition, symptom, and anxiety*, we know that we are anxious because we are inhibited, we are inhibited because we are afraid, fear of castration, fear of being ourselves, fear of following our impulses. Not even Freud himself dared to preach the liberation of the impulses. It was Wilhelm Reich who dared, after he became a militant for undoing repression.

Gestalt also fights against repression. Gestalt is Dionysian, it is a faith in mankind, the desiring self, the *it*, the It, which is a healthy part of our nature, although it must be integrated with others. Thus, fear must be reincorporated as one more of the capital sins.

In the other angle, on the right, we find Vanity. It does not appear on the list of sins because it is found near Pride and for some it seems that Pride and Vanity are the same thing. Nonetheless, the difference is clear in this oral tradition that I began to write down. Vanity means to focus too much on the gaze of others, to need those approving glances from other people too much; generally, a person with a lot of vanity discovers that they do not exist without other people, without the gaze of another person, they do not feel they have worth except in someone else's eyes, because they have no measuring stick, no intrinsic pattern of values; this is therefore, a person who depends heavily on the marketplace. David Reisman wrote a book called *The Lonely Crowd*: people who are very driven by what others will say, as if they had antennae for detecting the market of human values, from "this is how it's done" to "this is how you have to dress," fashion sense and setting the pace with others.

Pride, on the other hand, is an inflation of the person him/herself, in which one does not know one's own limits, lacks and needs and moves through the world like someone who gives. It is a good strategy to be in the love market: whoever is not in the love market, whoever is in a period of searching for a new love, will probably choose someone who has an excess of love. One could think that there are people who lack love and others who have a surfeit. How attractive those people who have too much of it are! They have enough to give, they are so loving. The problem is that they feel so loving by denying their need for love. It is as if they transform the idea of their own need for love into an "Oh, how much I need someone to receive my love!" They do not recognize: "How much I need someone to love me," when the vast majority of mortals need someone who loves them.

Sloth also is understood in another way; when the first monasteries were created, the idea of Sloth was formulated as what is commonly understood as such: someone who does not want to do this or that, someone who does not want to move or work much. However, that is not the laziness described by the Desert Fathers, who were very introspective and did not live in a situation of communal work as in the period of the first monasteries. If I am a hermit who is searching for God, I need to be in my cell praying; the principle is to not move from my cell, in case God comes to see me; if I am not in my cell, bad luck; therefore, I must stay there! The Desert Fathers realized that for some monks, the enemy was not Pride or Envy, all those inner enemies that can be located and grappled with but a much subtler enemy: the monks' loss of will to be there. "The Noonday Demon," Sloth is called. Or also acedia, a name that comes from the Greek word *akedia*, absence of caring.

The absence of care toward oneself is like not valuing oneself. It is as if while looking for something fundamental, one suddenly loses the will to do so. How can one compete against this demon of apathy, of slovenliness? It is like the power going off: there are people who lose it. Gurdjieff spoke of the demon of self-pacification, as if one pacifies oneself saying: "Don't exaggerate, resign yourself, don't complicate things." People who do this are very altruistic, but they do not give themselves what they need. It would seem that it is very Christian to be generous with one's neighbor and not to care about oneself but that is not true: that is not the Christian mandate. The Christian precept says: "Love thy neighbor as thyself." One cannot love thy neighbor without a basis of love of oneself. Something similar happens on airplanes: when there are problems, the instructions order you to place the oxygen mask over your own mouth before helping others. One must have that basis: if there is no love for oneself, how can one profess love for others?

Nonetheless, there is a popularized version of Christianity that says, "Don't love yourself." There are people who have the intention of being so good that their sin is not loving themselves: they are excessively self-sacrificing, and the problem is that whoever receives that love, does not receive it well. If someone has had a self-sacrificing mother, one of those who sacrifice everything for their child, they will understand. In the film *The Fiddler on the Roof*, a man sings to his wife, "Do you love me?" And the woman answers him, "I iron your shirts and I do this and that." And the husband asks her again, "But... do you love me?" There are people who are self-sacrificing by duty but not in the depths of their heart. They offer the love of a nanny, of a nursemaid, who lacks the touch of intimacy of heart of motherhood, that deep link of empathy; there are people who feel suffocated when they are given too many things and too much help but at the same time, lack that basic empathy.

So, we have these three primary colors in the central triangle: Vanity places a false self before others; Cowardice does not show the true self; and Confusion, blindness, becomes robotic and falls into automatic behavior. These are great explanations of neurosis. We could say that this triangle explains the dynamic of neurosis: as we are afraid we put on a mask, a representative to go out into the world, as we put on a mask we end up forgetting what is behind the mask, we become robotic, alienating ourselves; as we alienate ourselves, we feel weak, we do not have any anchors in ourselves, we are afraid that if we look deep within we will discover that we *do not exist*, that we are not there. Ronald Laing, the father of anti-psychiatry, said that the deepest fear is to look within oneself and discover that one is not, that we are a void.

The base consists of these three primary colors but mixing them forms the other colors. From any pair of points on the triangle, one can create two mixtures. Between blue and yellow, green is produced, which is neither blue nor yellow but a new quality; thus, between Vanity and Sloth two combinations are produced, one with more Vanity than Sloth and the other with more Sloth than Vanity. They have different characteristics: one is Anger and the other is Pride. Anger has something of blindness: it is said that Anger is blind; Pride has much Vanity, but it is not pure Vanity, since it has something of Anger. Pride places itself above the other; it acts superior, in a similar way to how the first point, Anger, corresponds to an authoritarian nature that protests and demands, in order to achieve what it wants.

All the sins are quite well known, although they are only partly understood, because they should be understood in a broader sense than usual. Many films have been made about the capital sins and generally the scene that corresponds to Gluttony is very silly. One cannot understand how getting up at night and stealing a cake can be compared to the sin of killing. Anger seems much worse, while Gluttony seems inconsequential. In reality, Gluttony is a confusion of pleasure with the meaning of life. There are people who deviate from living their own life because it is too comfortable. The search for pleasure is not, therefore, a simple search for pleasure, but a flight from pain. There are people who want to avoid the asperities of life and because they do not want to bother to truly live, they prefer to dream. Dreaming would not seem to be a particularly grave sin, but at some moment of life one reaps the fruit of having been only a dreamer and no one feels good not making the best of themselves, realizing that they wasted time dreaming.

Similarly, Lust does not have a strictly sexual meaning but is instead a passion in the broadest sense: a passion for intensity. Many people lose themselves in their overly large appetite for the flavor of intensity, they are bored with less intense things. Once, I wanted to present some ideas on computer and a hippie assistant told me that I had to add a flashing orange light to keep people more stimulated; there is a generation that no longer reads unless it is in very short little bursts because they do not have sufficient attention span and what little there is must be roused with strong and intense stimuli. The rock era generated a sort of spoiled mind, based on a "stimulate me" attitude.

So those are the sins and one could think that they are not going to make the world fall apart either, that their knowledge does not offer us anything that we did not already know in some way. All of us, more or less, have defects that we recognize. Reinterpreting them a little by placing them on this map is nothing sensational: it would not have been reason enough to produce this phenomenon of the famous Enneagram. What has been a success is the idea that for each negative emotion, for each passion, as Ichazo called it (that was one of his contributions, not talking of sins but passions) for each one of these deficient motivations that trap us because they are passions that want to fill a void, there is an associated *idea loca*: an irrational idea.

This is not merely a case of a timid person who may have inherited this fear from having had an overprotective mother who told him, "Be careful, don't fall." One can have been raised fearful because of having an insecure mother who went through very traumatic situations, who never felt protected and who transmitted and infected the child with a feeling of vulnerability. According to this vision, the passions do not run the deepest: what are called sins, those deficient emotional states, are pursued by an irrational idea. In the case of Fear, it is something like an antagonism toward oneself, a conviction that one has in the basement of the psyche something like a repulsive crocodile. That is the Freudian vision of the mind: one has something horrible inside, something ugly, something violent. When Freud wrote *Civilization and Its Discontents*, he did not dare to state that civilization was pathogenic because he suspected that it could be necessary to control our dangerous animal nature. Freud maintained that vision that we are dangerous animals, both good and bad and that it was better to teach us to be good through education and upbringing. In general, the humanist movement has been overcoming these ideas and over time, the idea has predominated that we do not need to live with a policeman in our heads and that a happier state results if we surrender ourselves to what is sometimes called *organismic self-control*, which is more or less what the Chinese call the Tao: the Law of Nature. We are very well built to coordinate ourselves. The mechanism of fear tells us that there is something to fear: the enemy, the serpent, temptation, desire; civilization is built on the premise that nature is not to be trusted, that our animal nature must be tamed: we are a self-domesticated species, after we domesticated the animals we did the same to our children so they would not bother us and of course, for their own good. I once saw a documentary about some tribes along the Amazon in which the young boys pierce their mouths and insert a reed that looks like a white beard. I do not know how it must feel to have that reed inside one's mouth. It seems to me that it would be a torture that all the adults get used to enduring with certain dignity and a person who does not have that reed is an incomplete human. I think that we are a little like that: we have inserted many things into ourselves based on the idea that we are not very well built as we are. All civilization is a movement to control and exploit nature but with very little faith in it. Nature is not even allowed to operate in childbirth: natural childbirths no longer exist, we have technological births where not even the woman has the right to decide how to give birth, at least unless she fights tremendously for it. They inject hormones, anesthesia, change the natural rhythms, cut the umbilical cord prematurely from the children, then give them a pat on the back so that they breathe. There are even a percentage of deaths, previously of unknown origin, which are now known to be caused by those micro bruises on the spine. In short, medicine has introduced a great furor, having great faith that this is necessary, as if we wanted to educate ourselves from the very womb to not trust nature, to feel that we need technology close at hand. This is the irrational element of one of the components of the Enneagram: Fear. We would not be afraid if we thought that we lived in a benevolent universe and that people were good. Of course, people have gone bad but it is one thing to have the vision that we are fallen angels or sick angels and another to think that we are structural devils. It is more beneficial to think that we come from a pure world, that we fell from paradise and were infected by a systemic evil. Thus, since Christianity said the Earth belongs to the Devil, it is fairly certain that there is a systemic evil:

we are all infected by these generalized vices. Some years ago, I was on the examining commission in a Spanish university, of a person who had written their doctoral thesis on the capital sins. One of the examiners said that without them, one could not work in a company, that they were indispensable for modern life. He said that virtue is pasé, but that is a tangent for another time.

How am I going to conclude this presentation on sins? I should explain what the irrational ideas of the nine points of the Enneagram are. I have said that fear is associated with an attitude of being at war with nature, which transforms into a war against oneself or against one's fellows.

At point one, Anger is connected with something that I have named Perfectionism. We are all a little bit perfectionist, perhaps but this is perfectionism in a pure state. Quino had a few comic strips about someone who is painting the edge of a road with a series of notices: honor, honesty, cleanliness, etc. In the act of painting these glorious affirmations, we understand that he is someone who does not have these qualities but who is attributing them to himself.

This idea was first formulated by Freud based on what in psychoanalyses came to be called the anal nature: people who have prematurely been educated in controlling their sphincters. Every child reaches a moment when they control themselves but if we wish to impose too much cleanliness on a child who still has not come to develop this control, they feel a failure, they will feel that they soil themselves, they will feel the burden of being a child who dirties things and who will be punished for being dirty. That is why Freud said that those who had that battle with their sphincters because they had parents who were overly perfectionist or controlling or complaining or demanding were going to be people who later would want to be compulsively clean. There are people who are so well educated, so obsequious, so attentive, so etc. They are like Boy Scouts: they do so many good deeds every day, they belong to the society of protection of animals, are members of the Red Cross, worthy representatives of good causes, etc. However, one sees that these people are, deep down, full of anger and when realizing that they are full of anger, they want to try and turn things around, as if they have to atone for something they have in excess.

I had a mother who did not want me to play with tin soldiers, so I would not become violent but as a child, I hated her and did not know why. I felt that I was being completely unfair but as an adolescent, I began to realize that she had squashed my spontaneity. Thus, a wrathful person wants to have lofty ideals and is someone who fights for good causes, but it turns out that those ideals do not coincide with what life wants. If one places a perfectionist woman in front of a child, she drives them crazy, "Don't put your feet there, that's not how you should say it, you didn't say thank you..." There are people who want to arrange things so much that they end up spoiling everything. I had a friend who said: "There are people who go too far varnishing the butterfly!" Varnishing the butterfly! Butterflies have marvelous colors; how would one varnish a butterfly? There are people who adorn gardens, they are manicurists of gardens; instead of understanding that trees and bushes already have beautiful natural forms, they want to impose forms on them. That is what Perfectionism is like.

In the case of enneatype two, Pride, the Christian world considered it to be the first of the sins. I think that theologians placed it as the first and most serious of sins because in truth it seems that the opposite were true: those who are proud treat themselves very well, they feel very good about themselves, they feel themselves to be implicitly superior to others, they do not feel that they lack anything. What inconvenience is there in feeling proud, feeling above others? I think that the problem of Pride is a spiritual problem: someone who is very full of himself does not grow; someone who is too satisfied with their life does not search; someone who feels grand does not pay attention to others who are grand, does not have a guide, does not have the power to admire, does not have a sense of what is above their own head. It is a sin that leaves people very much in this world: they do not go to psychotherapy, except when their partners leave them; generally, they go because of broken relationships.

In the case of point three of the Enneagram, Vanity consists of identifying oneself with the image that one sells. It is an error of perspective, a belief in what my inner advertising department says that I am. Just as there is a kind of beggar who injures their hands and cultivates wounds to seem more miserable and evoke more pity, in the United States that does not exist: one cannot declare that one does not earn enough; it is only thought that those who have more money are more successful. I once saw a cartoon in which an American beggar had a sign that read: "Earning, but not enough."

After the right corner of the Triangle, at point four we find Envy. It is a feeling that there is something one is missing and that another has. There are furious envies like that of Cain; there are people like that, who are furious because of what they do not have and others' privileges: women furious about the privilege that men have, poor people furious about the privileges that the rich have etc. Although a reaction of protest against injustice is justified, there are people who wallow in the pain and fury. Nonetheless, there is also a type of envy that suffers what is lacked by crying in excess, too much, becoming depressed by what it does not have. It is like those children who invent illness so as not to go to school or to receive a little more affection and to attract attention because of what they are missing. We can all be a little bit like fours, but there are people who make great use of this cultivation of the lack, of the complaint. In a complaint, there is a plea for love; we do not realize when we get depressed that in fact, we are the ones who throw ourselves to the ground. If we knew it, depression would not be so serious, if we know that we depress ourselves we could rescue ourselves from the depression. So, envy has to do with suffering too much: there are many people who suffer too much and who feel helped when they discover that this suffering is based on a way of perceiving things that is too comparative.

The fifth point, Greed, has to do with a vision of life in which one does not really believe in love. The person did not have a sufficiently strong tie with one of their parents, generally the mother. They do not know that this phenomenon of love exists; they do not know what is lost on not entering into a sufficiently close relationship. It seems a good thing to be alone in the world: one does not need to make so many compromises, give and take, come to an agreement about things, "let's see how we'll do this, if we're going to make this decision or an other." For a five, it is very difficult to negotiate with someone else, why bother? If one can be solitary, it is much easier, and they do not know that there is a dimension of life in which union exists. When there are two people, it is not just a case of adding one plus one, rather it passes to another level of existence. Nonetheless, a greedy person remains with a view of the world from the standpoint of poverty: "I have nothing to give and why am I going to get anything if there is nothing, I could get anyway... No doubt the people who make loving gestures toward me are people who want to manipulate me or trick me..." It is what today is called a schizoid nature.

The nature of those who are moved primarily by fear is more difficult to describe in view of their presenting in three rather different varieties: the insecure person, who is a timid idealist and needs affection; the fanatic who, on the contrary, is too sure of what they think and do (like Don Quixote) and the kind of people who in psychoanalysis have been called counterphobic, who are mistrustful and aggressively defend themselves against imaginary threats. All of them need to develop greater confidence in themselves, in their resources and abilities and in life itself.

Seven, Gluttony, is the fox of the fable. His case is a bit like what happens with the schizoid: someone who lives according to their own interests, very opportunist, who looks to take advantage of situations but with a great friendliness that masks all of this and he does not know what he is missing in human relationships, in the cultivation of the ability of surrendering oneself to another. It is, in short, a manipulative nature.

The Eight is a nature that has to do with Lust, with intensity. One could think: having a tendency toward intensity could be a vice, it could complicate life a little but when one sees that the philosophy of life that accompanies Lust is an exaggerated rebellion, it does not seem so serious. If we are in a domesticating society, on which castrates the children that we were, in a society that does not encourage the development of whole beings and that instead leaves us without wings, without initiative, without contact with our inner self, which impoverishes us, then those who rebel seem to be in the right. There are young kids who do not want to know anything about school or authority; they mistrust the principle of authority while most of us automatically submit to it and do not dare to distrust so much. While the majority thinks, "That's how the world is," the Lustful are rebels who think that, although they are in the minority, they are right, and we are all wrong. They think that it is not good to be as good as we want to be: to them, we are hypocrites. They think that they are the truly brave ones, that they realize how ugly and ill- intentioned people are. Sometimes they go a bit too far and sometimes they go way too far and end up involved in criminal activities; nonetheless when they do not cross over to crime, it is hard to not sympathize with them. Of the characters created by Shakespeare, one of the most popular was the famous Falstaff, from *Henry IV*, a noble buffoon who says everything that crosses his mind, who criticizes the kings and laughs at the aristocracies. Verdi also wrote an opera about *Falstaff*, where everyone is in sympathy with the protagonist because he laughs at all the social conventions. In the world of film, the equivalent would be *Zorba the Greek*. Zorba can trick people, but he is a good man; he ignores all the rules but his heart is in the right place. One of the spiritual masters of the 20th century, Osho, identified with Zorba: he referred to himself as Zorba the Buddha. There is some truth in the notion of mistrusting the world, but there is a nature called paranoid: which describes a person who takes that mistrust too far.

Nine seems so benign. They are lacking a love of themselves, but they are self-sacrificing. A mechanism of defense is at work in them which Freud called the altruistic surrender. Freud himself said that it is a healthier defense than others, which does no wrong, which makes everyone feel helped. However, not taking into consideration the person who has this compulsion of giving everything, does not come off very well. Only they do not know that they are not coming off very well. People who surrender are people who resign themselves to giving everything, who have nothing for themselves and do not know that their life has been impoverished.

So, what is to be done with all this? Something magnificent happens when people discover what their issue is. We all know that we have personality problems, problems with human relationships. Where there are relationship problems there are personality problems, but to locate this point so precisely, what is the passion, what is the associated idea, what we call the fixation, has many effects. It is as if it were a drop of some corrosive substance: you place it on the table and it begins to create a whole, you begin to make holes in your psyche, you begin to dismantle something. Few people have realized in their lifetime that they were wrong. It is a great experience when one comes to a moment of life in which you can say: "I have always been pursuing that, but that is not what I should be pursuing, my path lies elsewhere." This is called *metanoia*: a changing of one's mind or a conversion, if we use the religious reading. However, the conversion is treated very superficially, like adopting a system of beliefs. The real part of the conversion, the essence of the conversion, is a change of direction.

There is a myth that gave shape to an oratorio by Schumann: *Paradise and the Peri*. In the Mohammedan tradition, Peri is an angel who was cast out of Paradise with the mission of finding the bravest man on earth; only when he returns with said man will the gates of Paradise open again for him. It is told that Peri returns with the blood of a hero who has given his life in a battle, but he is informed that this was not the bravest man. He returns and wanders the earth until he comes back with a tear of love from a person who gave everything for the person he loved. The doors still do not open. Finally, he returns with a tear of repentance. The moral of the story is that realizing is the bravest thing of all. To see that one was wrong and to change direction. It is just that the word repentance is also very manhandled by Ecclesiastical authorities. There are too many calls to repent but the feeling is a great human experience: "Oh, now I see, it's not along here, but along there." Since that is accompanied by a desire for reparation, a desire to cultivate what is needed to emerge from that trap.

Not long ago, I was giving a conference to a group of businessmen and I asked who among them had experienced the feeling that they were wrong, of being able to understand this. A few of them raised their hands and one came to me afterwards, because he wanted me to dedicate a book to him. He told me, "I was wrong." and I asked him, "What was your error?" He answered, "I wanted to be a great business-man." "And now?" "Now I want to be a great man."

The majority of us have forgotten to be a person above all. Seeking is valued little in our culture. Those who seek are considered restless youth, who are not very appreciated and not well guided. I think that we will conclude this talk here. I have nothing more to say. Shall we finish slowly? Well, then... repent of your sins! [laughter] Trust yourselves.

I have told you that I do not think that this information that I have given you will be of much use if we separate it from its context, from a search for meaning. This tradition that is the search for this knowledge has been called on occasions the Fourth Way, meaning that it is a path that involves an element of action, an emotional part, a mental part and a fourth part that is working on attention. When I have wanted to use the Enneagram, I have used it as an element within this mosaic: a very broad mosaic. I regret that it has become an independent profession because the Americans, who became enthusiastic with this teaching, got themselves together and created a professional association, the International Association of the Enneagram, which, as a professional organization, set itself up as a valid institution for teaching the Enneagram, although it does not have much capacity to lead others through a transforming process. To develop that capacity, one needs to reach a special spiritual fulfillment or to have a rather solid therapeutic training. So I would like to go further in this matter: the starting point for transformation is to watch oneself and doing so through the day to day is very difficult. The day distracts us from the attitude of the observer; it is necessary to observe oneself for at least a short while every day, without moving, without doing things, and that is what we call meditation: to be with oneself, to be with oneself in an attitude of observing the moment itself. There we begin to see more.

The Desert Fathers were hermits who did not live in relation to others. Those who cultivated this thinking, who developed something so important, were hermits who looked at themselves alone in the stillness because they had this faith: a faith passed on from masters to disciples where, in order to find oneself with the experience of the divine, one had to pacify the passions. This consists of not feeding the ego. Epicure had already seen it: the great master of pleasure, the great preacher of the faith in pleasure, said that to have pleasure one must suffer less and in order to suffer less, one must not have so many desires, not have so much fondness for desires, one must simplify life, cultivate *apatheia*, a condition of neutral consciousness. That is the starting point: being with oneself in stillness. From there one begins to see and this map becomes clearer.

How does one work on oneself? The SAT Program, where self-awareness predominates, has the ambition of working on five things; The first is the liberation of erotic love: it is castrated and that is something which psychotherapy already contemplates but which was the oldest specialty of religions, since before the Gods of Olympus arose, in Greece the Dionysian religion already existed, based on faith in nature. So, the Dionysian spirit abounds in the SAT.

The second consists of the recovery of the ties of love. I spoke of parents as a starting point because, as the Fourth Commandment says, "honor thy father and mother." This is a good item in a system of rules for life on planet Earth:

if we want to recover those ties, because most of us have inconclusive, festering, forgotten issues, we must reopen our old wounds in order to investigate the past and look at what happened with our father and mother. If we want to evolve, have a larger heart, more capacity for love, we must look back at those outstanding issues.

The third is cultivating devotion. I think that it is a very important part of life: we do not just have a compassionate love that looks to our fellow humans but also a love that looks to the heavens. This does not need to be called a love of God: it can be called by a thousand different names, it can be called a love of Dharma, a love of the Tao, a love of the Path, a love of inner work etc. I think that the path to cultivating devotion is music. The sensation music gives us is much more than aesthetic: what thrills us in music is a mystery, it is a connection with the pinnacle, it is a crypto-religion. Therefore, in SAT IV and SAT V, the emphasis is on devotion.

Then comes awareness of character: psychological self-awareness.

Afterwards, there is deep self-awareness, which is also called wisdom. It sounds a little ambitious that a school that functions with a proposal of working only a few days a year, in such brief modules, concern itself with wisdom but wisdom is made up of self-awareness and detachment. Detachment is something very mysterious: in the mundane, in psychotherapy, there is no interest in detachment. It is a specifically spiritual phenomenon, that of giving things up. Giving up even such simple things as the past and the future to live fully in the present or giving up thinking that we are fixated on to the exclusion of everything else. We acquire detachment in life through the natural process of growing older: it is said that the elderly become wise, they look at life from a greater distance, with fewer attachments; nevertheless this process can be accelerated and this is done through meditation, giving up impulses, in a situation of mental stillness and silence.

That system goes very far: these are the coordinates, the ingredients of all the great spiritual movements of the world and I think that we need all of them. We need the three loves: the erotic, the admiring and the charitable. We also need the two extremes of knowledge: psychological self-awareness and that other deeper self-awareness that is sometimes called wisdom, which is what the Oracle of Delphi recommended when asking: "Who are you? Who are you really? Who are you really beyond your masks, beyond your ego?"

CHAPTER 7

Heading Toward Wisdom:

THE RECOVERY OF THE INTUITIVE MIND WITH THE HUMANITIES

WE HUMAN BEINGS HAVE PROCLAIMED ourselves to be Homo Sapiens but having done this is perhaps a sign of our limited wisdom, since it would be difficult for us to proclaim ourselves wise if we recognized our tragic ignorance.

I use the term ignorance here in the sense given to it by Buddha, Socrates, Saint Augustine, and others, rather than the one which our current educational institutions use, where it is usually confused with a lack of knowledge, or even a lack of information, now that we are more interested in literacy than in wisdom. This is so to such an extent that to talk of wisdom to a minister of education would surely be perceived as coming to him with utter pretentiousness that had little to do with his fundamental mission of teaching us the alphabet and the multiplication tables.

What is wisdom? That wisdom of the ancients from which the word philosopher (lover of wisdom) comes is something so unknown in the world today that not even the people in our cultural environment clearly understand what it is about. We barely understand that it has to do with a way of understanding things that the wise men throughout history have had access to: a way of understanding life that makes people naturally virtuous.

Although we intellectually understand that both Buddha as well as Socrates thought that ignorance is the cause of our suffering and our destructiveness, that does not mean that we understand what this wisdom is about, the absence of which defines our ignorance. We are surrounded by vast literature about wisdom and moreover all of the literature produced from wisdom, which we find both in the writings of the different spiritual traditions (from the Old Testament to the Sutras of Mahayana Buddhism) as well as in great literature and poetry. That is why sometimes humanist education hoped that it would be good for us to study the classics but now we have forgotten why the classics were studied, or what wisdom the classics could pass on, since we come to understand little beyond the literal and explicit meanings of the great epics, tragedies, or novels.

One could very well imagine the project of a transcultural anthology that would inspire in readers and especially in students a taste for wisdom and an approach toward its intuition. However, that would come nowhere near to leading us toward wisdom itself, which requires much more than doctrines, theological formulations or mystic commentaries about such things as emptiness and the Tao.

Buddhism says in its formulation of the Noble Eightfold Path, that the first aspect of the path toward illumination is a correct understanding of certain truths that are inaccessible without an experiential exploration and in an analogous way, we could say that wisdom is a way of perceiving and feeling by someone who has lived a path of transformation and not merely a rational apprenticeship.

The oldest of the literary works of humanity (the epic of Gilgamesh, which the Babylonians inherited from the Sumerians) offers us its hero as one who has reached wisdom and we understand through this that wisdom is nothing other than having walked the path to its end. But what do we modern people know of the path to wisdom?

We barely recognize that within our potential as human beings, lies that of passing through a sort of metamorphosis, which entails something like dying to the past and a rebirth into a higher consciousness. However, the culture in which we live today is one in which many will consider such an idea as mere superstition.

Therefore, I think that higher education should return the voice to the religious geniuses of the past, until now muzzled in the name of science and in a certain way to follow their advice in order for us to interest ourselves in that inner journey or path of transformation. This is a process of development of attention, of self-awareness, of liberation from our destructive emotions (the famous monsters of fairy tales and myths), as well as of unification among our inner voices in conflict; a process that culminates in the direct perception of certain truths that today have become simple philosophical opinions.

When wondering what an education for wisdom may be, this naturally involves confronting the core of the subject of an education for the spirit, which ironically has become as controversial a subject as whether education should interest itself in the emotional world. This controversy has resulted from the approach of a ridiculous alternative between providing people with the religion of their culture or educating them in an environment free from religious domination by this or that church.

Fortunately, people can be educated spiritually without the support of any religion, looking after that deep aspect of the mind that is consciousness itself. Going beyond the religious, in the sense that religion involves dogmas or codes of conduct, we could return to the fundamental fact of religions, which is the spirit itself. One can orient oneself toward the heart of this awareness of the spirit for the spirit that we call wisdom, through a series of exercises of self-awareness by practicing meditation aimed toward the cultivation of detachment and inner peace, which can be described without reference to any religious context. I let myself state this because over some forty years of explorations in psycho spiritual work with groups, I cannot doubt that the majority of my students have felt themselves progress along the path of psychological awareness that is at the same time one of delving deeper into contemplative experience, work that has been evaluated by people at the universities of Barcelona and London with results that are just a pale reflection of the gratitude felt by the participants themselves.

It is said that there are many paths but the hegemonic spirit of our culture has until now blocked us from creating a curriculum of integrative meditation that serves the maturation of the educators and here I will just say that I have no doubt that this is possible, simply because I have been offering it to the teachers and therapists who come to my programs year after year. Just as I say that it is not necessary to bring conventional psychotherapy to schools, since what is important is the understanding of the therapeutic process,

I insist that it is also not necessary to bring any religions to schools, which are just sociopolitical phenomena derived from wisdom in a patriarchal world. No matter how they have tried to appropriate the spiritual life of the community, it is now time that we get to the essence: a spiritual education that begins with a certain familiarization with the thinking of the wise men of different cultures (without excluding the fairy tales), which is deepened through transforming self-awareness and which culminates in the practice of silence and detached stillness.

Given that I have considered self-awareness and recommended that the voices of the religious geniuses of mankind be heard again, in the next chapter I propose to explain the potential of meditation in the context of a future education. As a first step, it seems relevant to me to explain how the monopoly of science in our time has interfered not just with traditional religious faith but also with the working of our intuitive abilities, indispensable for the understanding of human issues.

After the discovery during the 1960s of how the production of Alpha waves in the electroencephalogram of those who meditate (shortly after a relationship between trance states with theta waves was also observed), this information had a very large impact. However, to me it seems rather ridiculous that the prestige of the electroencephalogram could surpass to such an extent that of awareness; especially seeing as how the electroencephalogram is a very approximate way of seeing, given that the average electrical activity of the brain is something very crude. It is like wanting to study the life of a city through the lights illuminated in it on one single night.

Later, things began to be seen in greater detail, for example: the consistence between the two hemispheres of the brain; other elements were also detected, like through magnetic resonance, the discovery that happiness has to do more with activity on the left side of the brain than the right, less activity in the tonsils etc. To me it never seemed that such things were important for science or for meditation. They are pieces of information added to the flow of scientific knowledge but not every increase in the flow of scientific knowledge is important for science as science.

To me, the question of how important meditation is for science makes me ask myself in turn what lesson science could learn from an approach to meditation with regards to its position: the scientific attitude or form of science is to approach the truth.

It seems to me that the principle is that just as we have the use of reason, we are also endowed with intuition and just as we have the possibility of studying consciousness through science, in other words, through intelligence, we also have the possibility of studying consciousness through consciousness–that is to say, to resort to the phenomenological method, which is also the experiential method.

To science in general, experience has not been worth much, it is considered purely subjective, not even intuition, except as a source of inspiration for the great inductions. Deduction is very easy; induction is very difficult, and intuition is necessary to achieve it.

Some time ago, a thick book by Steven Pinker about the mind captured my attention. After verifying that it contained very valid information, I searched the index to see what it said about consciousness and discovered that, despite being such a thick and important psychology book, it contained only two or three pages about the subject. Nonetheless, I found in these pages an idea that is very astute: an observation that eagles have very fine eyesight, that lets them see over a great distance what is happening on the earth and thereby locate their prey, even insects. However, in another sense, eagles are very awkward: they are practically deaf. Pinker makes the following analogy: "We humans have a very good eye for intellect but we do not have the right organ to understand consciousness." I liked that observation, which humbly recognizes a limitation of science.

Often people in the scientific camp feel that little is lost by disregarding that which reason does not know how to judge. Those in the world of intuition feel that the scientists lose a lot, because a person in who that other intuitive sense of life or sense of interiority is awake, being open to the path of experience, can approach that maturity that leads to wisdom and a full life.

The scientists do not have the assurance of having full lives. Even when they want to formulate thoughts about ethical, aesthetic, or religious matters, they always sound like second-hand thinkers, issuing opinions that could be like this or not. One reads what Kant says about aesthetics and it seems a little ridiculous to us. Or Hegel. The greatest philosophers say trivial things. On the other hand, what the saints say or those people whose lives are inspired by love, or the genius creators, we do value as first-hand. What Beethoven says about aesthetics is indeed an opinion we consider to be authorized, because it comes from the appropriate organ: the organ that could generate that music understands music.

Therefore, it seems to me that what remains to be learned by science in its eagerness for truth is to strip itself of its scientism. I call "scientism" that arrogance that historically developed in science when that famous confrontation against the faith that we associate with the Age of Enlightenment, during the time of Kant and Voltaire, took place. When their lucidity dethroned the kings and the limits of ecclesiastical authority were questioned as never before, rational thought felt liberated. But the only form that reason had of triumphing over arguments of faith (which were wrapped in ecclesiastical authoritarianism), was the development of a corresponding, opposing authoritarianism, and thus religious dogmatism was fought with a dogmatism of reason; of those who only believe in reason.

At the heart of those dogmatisms is the power of that authoritarianism which I have come to call patriarchal power. It would seem that the entire world was prisoner to a hegemonic attitude that is a vice from which no individual or culture escapes: "This is the Truth," some say, and others respond, "No, this is the Truth." "I am right." "No, I am right." There is little capacity for synthesis and little consideration that perhaps it would be healthy, in addition to obvious, that just as we have a left hemisphere and a right hemisphere, we have reason and we have intuition and it is not necessary to set them against each other thinking that one is the path of truth and not the other. Would it not be more promising to think that our cerebral hemispheres process the data of our lives and environment differently, in a similar way to our eyes, looking at objects from different directions allows us to have depth of vision? There are many, surely, who have lived this way. The best scientists: Schrödinger, William James etc.

William James believed in apparently crazy things, because he was a pragmatist. He did not pay too much tribute to scientific truth, in the sense of a concordance between this affirmation and that state of things: more important for him was the truth; that was what worked. His pragmatism consisted precisely of that: if it works to think that there is a higher world that envelops this one, fine, then it suits us to adopt this position in order to grow and to develop ourselves.

Although the great scientists have often been open-minded people, with enormous curiosity and a desire for knowledge not muddied by scientific dogma, in the scientific culture (given its prestige in our culture) there arose a sort of excrescence, which is an arrogance of reason that emerged as an opposition to the supposedly irrational, which was understood as being contaminated by power. Thus, in our secular culture one cannot use words like spirit or love, which in the academic world do not have the right tone and when things that are very important for life do not fit into the language, life ends up becoming more limited and language itself becomes a repressive element.

I think that the exaltation of science served greatly to defend itself from the oppression of the Church in another time and to promote freedom of thinking but at this moment, there is something anachronistic in this implicit dogma that only that which is scientific is valid, or only scientific views count.

Toward the end of my medical studies I wanted to write my thesis on the routes of innervation of the pineal gland. Wishing to elucidate what physiological manifestations could correspond to the anatomical connections, I turned to a renowned scientist of the time to loan me his team and let me work in his laboratory. Nonetheless, he wanted to convince me to instead study the nervous fiber isolated in a ganglion of the cockroach. I could have spent decades on it and like him, have also made great discoveries in the ganglia of the cockroach but I do not regret having followed a different path.

In science there is this tendency of "let us not aspire to things that are too difficult," "let us not look for the key there, where it is dark; we search better under the light of lamps, that is to say, under the light of the intellect."

It seems to me that today we are living a late but obsolete apogee of the mentality of Enlightenment. That Voltairean mentality, from the Age of Enlightenment, that was important in its time but which has been questioned since then by the Romantics, the Existentialists, the Structuralists and the Post-structuralists, has triumphed in the world of politics and economy, which places its greatest hopes in science and technology, with the result that cultures, entire peoples, values, etc., are all destroyed. Why say it: something is wrong with that unilaterality of the scientific-technological approach.

Surely, our time of comets and earthquakes is one in which the old prophets of Israel would instruct people to consider the consistency of their acts with divine will. Now that we live in a period in which we do not believe in either prophets or *God* (in italics, as that word has been used in vain so much that it has lost its worth), perhaps God should not be invoked but instead something that makes us think more, like the Tao.

Tao is a Chinese term that has two translations: "Nature" and "path" and the notion of Tao is one which has recently been entering psychotherapy through the concept of organismic self-regulation. Jesus said: "I am the Way, the Truth, and the Life" but I think that before a Chinese tribunal he would have said: "I am the Tao"—because whoever enters the Tao no longer has an individual existence, instead it is the Tao that lives through him.

From our usual perspective we forget that we are agents of life, that we are part of a larger existence, comparable to pseudopods of a cosmic existence. Perhaps we knew it during our embryonic state but in our accustomed state we are more like the famous fly of the proverb that said "Let us plow" when it had barely alighted on the horn of the ox. Just as the fly thought, we also think that we are the owners and agents of our lives, when life happens independently of our intentions and we are much more automatic than we think. The Tao is the non-self. It is life. Or it is the heart of life, the essence of life.

Just as it is said that the world comes from the Tao, which is split into Yin and Yang, from which ten thousand things spring, and that the world heads toward the Tao and is never separated from it, in our modern world the notion of the Buddhahood is also beginning to solidify. This is the energy of awakening and the possibility that the fundamental reality is consciousness itself is beginning to be considered. Not even in physics are the material phenomena separated from the observer, in whose absence reality becomes a great mystery. "Probabilities," it is said. But these waves of probabilities are not waves of a material medium and therefore through them many scientists who have become interested in meditation have become familiar with Buddhism. To anyone who approaches Buddhist culture, the idea that Buddhahood is the supreme purpose of life begins to rub off on them and that could smooth out a sort of fanatic barbarian spirit that was adhering to science as a residue of an expired patriarchal culture.

That influence would indeed have consequences for culture and not just for the life of the scientists (whose minds could be enriched if they became interested not just in knowledge but also in wisdom). Our culture continues to divide itself into two camps and we are educated under a presupposition that just as one must choose between Daddy and Mommy, one must also choose between reason and intuition, or between rationalism and experientialism.

In psychology, experientialism is on the rise: the great psychological discoveries have come out of an experiential root; for example, those of Freud, which arose from the couch and not from abstract thought.

In fields like this, faith in experience and intuition are entering and we will be more complete human beings if we reach the full dignity of our complete nature, if we do not have to choose between intuition and science, which is like choosing between our left and right brains, according to a now-obsolete and impoverishing dichotomy.

Therefore, it would be opportune for education to again interest itself in the humanities, thereby fostering access to the intuitive abilities that underlie and favor wisdom, in a comparable manner to how becoming interested in freedom will propitiate the development of empathy, and becoming interested in self-awareness will favor the development of love.

CHAPTER 8

The Potential of Meditation:

EDUCATION OF THE SPIRIT BEYOND RELIGIONS

O NE ASPECT OF MEDITATION is stillness; stopping the current of thought. We are always in movement, we are always doing this or that and we do not realize that our compulsion to do things, a subtle compulsion to generate thoughts, is also a compulsion to want to fill the void of our being with something past or future: the next movement, the next thing, the next project, the next achievement, and so on.

Centuries ago, Pascal said that the world's problem is that people do not know how to stay quietly in their own rooms, and I think that there was more reason in that than is usually understood. There is within every person a lack of peace and the corresponding inability to be satisfied with oneself, and with life, that is profoundly relevant to the peace of the world.

Stillness is a meditative practice that has many forms and we find it in many traditions: in Hinduism, Buddhism, Taoism, Sufism, and Christianity. The Fathers of the Church thought that those who could not reach silence could not have access to communion, which is to say that there is no encounter with the divine if one does not first obtain a silent mind. That was Saint John of the Cross' specialty, and Saint Teresa recruited him as the most competent educator of the novitiates when she founded the Carmelite Order.

Naturally, the practice of stillness does not just involve the body but also our thinking. Someone who tries to let their thinking rest discovers that the obstacle for that is emotional agitation: a state of being in search of this or that. Our excessive agitation has its roots in the world of neurotic needs or passions, which is nothing other than what the ancients called the sins. A person who has too much ambition, for example, cannot remain still, since an ambitious person is someone who is always struggling toward their project, creating something or imagining possible futures and staying still leads them to feel they are losing time. Neither can an envious person remain still, and all those sins that the ancients recognized have in common the problem of distancing us from the peace of stillness. Therefore, we can say that the practice of stillness is like a panacea: it cures all our automatic compulsions, according to our specific type of ego (or different types of psychological machinery). Although the dominant motivations in various types of people are different, in such a way that we could say that there are cowardly minds, lazy minds, lustful minds (which always look for intensity in order to feel alive), pampered minds (which want to feel that everything is warm and cozy, since they search for both pleasure as well as the compulsive avoidance of displeasure), all of them lose something of their power in people who try to distance themselves from their thinking. In fact, someone who lives completely wrapped up in their thoughts does not see beyond them and loses contact with their experiences. Ordinary life is a condition in which we are so absorbed in our memories, our anticipations of the future and in our commentaries about life, that we are not even living the present.

Above all, we are not living that aspect of the present that is simply being or being *here*. To be present, merely feeling our existence, seems of little interest to us. That being present is not very highly valued in today's world, when what is valued above all is information and that which is practical. Simply being has no practical value and only those who begin to evolve internally begin to evaluate being present or knowing themselves to be present. Sometimes I find myself with people who answer my question "What are you looking for in life?" with "To be in the here and now," and that deep interest in being in the here and now seems to me to be a sign of unusual maturity.

I once took part in a forum on education with someone who practiced Zen Buddhism and when someone in the audience asked him, "Who is God for you?" I liked his unusual response: "I think that God is the seizing of the present moment, that we only feel vaguely and with delay." That is to say: God escapes from us from moment to moment and God is an intuition of what we feel deep within our being, which in truth belongs neither to us nor to anyone but is simply Being. This not escaping from the present through the work of the imagination is a doorway to that sensation of existing that we value so little in comparison with our projects and our ambitions but it is at the same time the beginning of the discovery that life is sacred. If we do not have contact with our Being, we do not have contact with the Being of anyone. Everything is then transformed into thoughts, abstractions, things, etc.

Stillness, then, is a large doorway. A doorway to something that in the end is a mystery, because we have not lived it yet. A door that seems to be something like what water is to fish, which it is said they do not perceive it, precisely because they live in it. There is nothing more familiar than "we ourselves," the subject of our own consciousness that has become invisible to us because of its familiarity. If we cultivate that "I am," however, watering it with our attention like a little plant that is given water every day, it becomes not just a source of peace but also of great wellbeing. A peace that is not the absence of conflicts but something like an inner strength that can endure even in the midst of the agitation of our conflicts.

Education for peace seems to me to be a very important human need but we must understand that the peace of the world requires inner peace. It would be a very important gift for any person to be able to achieve a greater tranquility simply by finding themselves alone with the unmoving depths of the mind itself, instead of being lost in the multiplicity of their impulses and the abstractions of thinking.

What would it cost to do this? It would be necessary for there to be enough people who understood the issue and for initiatives to arise in this regard, but it is difficult to have initiatives in the large bureaucracies. I have always said that education seems like an enormous white elephant to me: the most difficult to move perhaps, among all bureaucracies. We know that the great bureaucracies begin by serving something but end up only serving themselves. It is a great sociological problem.

I will not dwell too much on peace, trusting that someday it will be understood that it comprises an important, neglected subject of education.

It is not only of interest to know how and be able to remain still, leaving the mind in repose by silencing our thinking. Also of interest is what would appear to be the complete opposite: to let the mind flow, since we are life and as living organisms, our mind is also part of the process of life. However, we are not truly free to let life flow spontaneously in ourselves. Children, who have not yet lost their spontaneity and initiative, are freer than we are but little by little they become domesticated and education takes care of making them just like us. They lose their happiness as well, through the process of domestication to which they are subjected, particularly in view of happiness not being contemplated among the goals of education.

Human happiness will depend one day on our becoming interested in the happiness of the children and it is a shame that what was the program of the great wise men in Greece is not in the political vision of today. Lycurgus, Solon and Plato shared the idea that one could not aspire to a happy community without being concerned with creating virtuous people and what they understood by virtuous was something very different from our morality. Virtue for them was rather an inner state from which to naturally do good; which implies that we are naturally good if we are well and that destructiveness comes from an interference with our nature, that is to say, from our circumstantial plagues.

It is interesting then, to not just cure by silence and attention to the depths of our consciousness but also cure through freedom and obedience to our true life that we are not living because of all kinds of interferences. We do not live Life, nor can we say that we are in harmony with Life. The processes of domestication, education, and upbringing have alienated us, and technological birth has already removed us from contact with the belief in nature that should inspire us.

It is clear that in the world today it is thought that the fetus, like animals, has very little awareness. Nonetheless if one imagines that the fetus is conscious, one would not be so indifferent to the medical profession that separates a newborn from its mother, or asphyxiates it a little when it prematurely cuts the umbilical cord (in view of the doctors being very busy and rushed), or which pats the newborn on the back to provoke a cry.

Although there is barely a 0.5 percent possibility of complications in natural births, it is very revealing that in South American countries, at least half of all births are via cesarean section. Apart from showing the despotism of culture over mothers, it also shows an interference with the natural order; consistent with the way in which the techno economic system appropriates our lives from the moment we are born, separating us from that natural order. Generally, it has been thought that nothing matters to the child, but I think that newborns, who still do not know the world, have not yet completely lost that awareness that we spend the rest of our lives looking for. Without knowing it, whoever searches for illumination, or the divine, yearns to recover the mind of the fetus, as Freud already thought, by maintaining that the oceanic states of mysticism involved recovering a memory of the fetal state. We must not think that to interpret it in that way (that we are part of the whole and that we once knew this) is to diminish the scope of our yearning. From being told so often "pay attention to this," "careful with that," "don't fall," "pay attention to what I am saying," etc., and through so many obligations, children are disconnected from that condition of simply being at peace and of knowing how to Be.

It would seem that this making way for life is the opposite of stillness, rather it is more a case of complementarity. It can be said that in meditation there is a dimension that goes from the red light (from the invitation to stop) to the green light (the invitation to flow) and those who meditate know very well that those are only incompatible conceptually. In Zen tradition it is usually said that one should let the mind be like the sky, unmoving and imperturbable, through which clouds pass; which is to say that even if one lets the mind itself be like the sky, which is pure space, that will mean that like space, it is permeable.

The healthier our mind is, the more permeable it will be and that will translate into our being more able to accept things and above all to accept our own experience of the moment. This also translates into being able to accept others, instead of feeling that we should be armed against imaginary or hypothetical threats to our way of being.

To say that we should give ourselves to the current of life, or to a greater spontaneity, is something that has a relationship with the trust that there is within us an organismic intelligence. During the past century, Cannon introduced the term homeostasis in reference to an elemental mechanism of biological self-regulation but much more broadly one can

speak of something like a wisdom of the instinctive. Our
mind has a much greater complexity than what the thinking
mind can embrace, so that we cannot navigate through life
letting ourselves be guided only by our rational mind. This
is known by those who speak of the characteristics of good
leadership in a company, or those who move in the business
world, which requires a good nose, that is to say, intuition.

I call this aspect of meditation the dimension of surrender. This surrender seems to be very present in the history of
religions, but misrepresented. The surrender to God, which
for a mystic means dissolving into the divine (and through
that, dissolving as well one's personal will into an obedience
of divine will, as in the phrase "Thy will be done" in the Our
Father), has historically been transformed into obedience to
the church, its emissaries and authorities. Divine will though,
does not pass through legislation or a code, even if it is one
as sublime as the Ten Commandments of Moses. For the
nature of the surrender is a state of permeability to a more-
than-human influence that does not move through verbal
or even conceptual mandates. Surely because the surrender
has been codified, making it an obedience to these or those
precepts of this or that religion (including above all those
which define themselves as the way of surrender, or Islam),

implies a betrayal by the religious authorities to the actual surrender, which is a giving up of control. A mandate of control is imposed therefore on the mind itself based on masked police-like demands.

Nietzsche said in the 19th Century that what the civilization of his time most needed (Christian culture in decline, with its moralist and repressive, inquisitorial spirit) was a reinjection of the Dionysian spirit that inspired the original religion of humanity.

No matter how central he had been to the original religion of Europe, since the Olympic gods were established, Dionysus came to be a marginal god among the Greeks. The era of his predominance was pre-patriarchal, and Alain Danielou says that Dionysus is none other than Shiva in India; this author cites a curious observation: when Alexander the Great invaded India, the initiates who traveled with him encountered the initiates in the mysteries of Shiva and they understood one another, recognizing that they were all part of the same school and brotherhood.

Today we associate Dionysus with pleasure; but pleasure is just one aspect of the Dionysian spirit. More fundamental is the surrender to spontaneity, which in turn entails a faith in nature, both internal as well as external, in contrast with the spirit of civilization that wishes to control, predict and exploit nature, taking advantage of it and domesticating it for goals that are alien to it.

In many ways, this cultivation of surrender can lead to its practice and one form of this is a type of meditation itself, in silence. But one can also give expression to this through the imagination (as in lucid dreaming) and even in the practice of giving free rein to thought, such as in the free association of psychoanalysis. Especially liberating is the surrender to spontaneous movement, as in the discipline of Authentic Movement, which is an invitation to let oneself be carried away by something unknown, beyond the small everyday self. We say of these moments in which something beyond our will comes into operation, that they are moments of inspiration, like in the activity of inspired artists.

I said that we could conceive of the path of surrender as complementary to the path of stillness and I would say that the more we achieve stillness (in other words, that which the Chinese call *wu wei*, the non-action, the being able to be without doing, not being slaves of the usual compulsive action), the greater depth and authenticity our lives will reach, which are ordinarily full of detours and tangents. Instead of really living our lives, we live many borrowed experiences and we live to a great extent by approximation and falsification. In summary, each of the poles of the complementary pair of "stopping/flowing" favors the other.

Another aspect of meditation is attention. In education, the word attention is used very often and it is said, for example that "attention must be paid." That is a very partial attention though that is only turned to a task, which is especially useful for productivity. Of greater interest for personal evolution is attention to the inner world. Socrates said that the Oracle had ordered him to question people about their knowledge of themselves, to concern himself with the issue of self-awareness; but there is no self-awareness without a previous contact with experience itself. We do not even know to what degree our awareness is limited by what we feel.

There would be no psychotherapy if it were not for this phenomenon, which we alluded to with the term *repression*. Psychotherapy is needed to return to a person what could be their birthright or natural ability: knowing what they feel.

We all think we know what we feel, but according to therapeutic experience we are rather far off the mark. Sometimes we think we feel one thing and we feel the opposite, sometimes we have no idea what we want. It still is hard for us to discover our true desires, and it is also part of the job of psychotherapy to help people recover their true desires, which are usually forbidden or censured, because since we were children we have been made to feel that it was not acceptable to desire this or that. We lose the spontaneity of expression of our desires, to the degree that we no longer know them ourselves. And the unawareness of our impulses goes hand in hand with their criminalization. Even in this historic period of apparent sexual freedom, in which it seems that the famous Victorian morality of Freud's day were something from another time, people are very far from being free when it comes to sex. If this were not the case, there would be no pornography, which responds to a pleasure of the forbidden that is like the obsession to get even.

There would be more happiness as well, if there were a deep harmony with our desires and impulses. It is as if there were in us the residue of an original *no*: the experience of our inner child, who has been told "don't," "don't," and "don't" so many times: "Don't touch," "Don't do," "Don't look for," "Don't say. . ." This produces a search for freedom on another level, which does not manage to undo that sensation that deep down there is something dirty, something ugly, something which one should control before it is expressed, looked at, or inspected.

Psychotherapy looks to recover such things, beginning with the discovery (especially in psychoanalysis) of what we think. In psychoanalysis, through free association, one sees what one thinks and shares with another who is observing what goes through the mind: the ideas, the fantasies, the considerations. Thus one becomes familiarized with one's thinking and letting oneself be guided by a sort of detective (who is the analyst) through one's underlying motivations.

This comprises an education, but it can also be considered a very basic form of education, which is simply attention to what one is going through in the present moment. Attention to the here and now.

In the culture we are a part of, we do not realize to what degree we are not aware of the here and now. There is not a lot of here and now in our conversation, not even when someone asks another: "How are you?" One answers automatically without thinking, without looking. If we were to answer sincerely, very often we would say, "Well... Look, in reality, I don't know how to say it. Well... I feel more or less fine, but... Mmmmm... My tone doesn't tell me that." We are not sufficiently aware to be able to express ourselves with enthusiasm about what it is that is going on here and now. Then, that connection fills up with the past, the future, and philosophizing about life, but not with life itself.

Attention to the present has that dimension of knowing what happens in the world of mental phenomena: feeling, wanting, thinking, etc. but not just that. Such attention would have a psychological benefit: knowing what one feels, what one wants, what one thinks; it would already be in itself a transformative self-awareness, little by little, because one takes to one's heels at the first sign of self-awareness. If you look in the mirror, you feel like combing your hair. If you look in the inner mirror, you feel like getting in better shape, getting a slightly better attitude.

But there is also another dimension of attention, which is neither attention toward the external world nor attention toward thinking, feeling, and loving, but rather attention toward the depths of the mind.

In meditation, we are not solely interested in "what it is I see" even if that is "I see mental phenomena, I see thinking, feeling, and loving" but instead "who is looking." There is an intent, an ambition in the discipline of meditation, to know the subject of consciousness. What in Buddhism is called the "inquiry into the nature of the mind." It is not a philosophical inquiry but an exploration of consciousness through consciousness itself, a phenomenological inquiry: something like wanting to see one's eyes, which is not physically possible for anyone to do. But in the spiritual world there is indeed a phenomenon along the lines of crossing a barrier. Although one does not normally find the subject of consciousness, a spiritual condition of self-reflectiveness does exist which is not seeing ones thoughts, or seeing one's mundane life, as it is called, but seeing the one who is looking, or rather encountering the deep "itself," which is our actual consciousness.

It is normally a long path. He who finds himself, finds the meaning of life, finds fulfillment and finds what is usually called the divine: that which has been called by so many names, such as Buddhahood, the inner Christ, the Tao, and so on. Every spiritual tradition has its own name for it. The Great Spirit. Its primary characteristic is the sacred. The deep contact with the center of ourselves is the contact with the sacred: which is something that everyone values just as we value beauty on an aesthetic level. It is like a form of nourishment, a spiritual nourishment, we could say. It is a marvelous feeling, which we have sometimes felt in one or another moment in life, but which has generally left us with just a taste.

We are not very familiar with holiness. There are certain people who give us a feeling of what holiness might be like; sometimes there are readings that make us feel that, or temples that might evoke it.

It has been said that meditation becomes a field in which to cultivate a sanctifying attitude that is like a form of creation that the ancients sometimes called theurgy, which means something like a creation of the divine through a different ability than ordinary imagination, what the sufis have called the creative imagination. In such cases one must visualize or evoke or invoke something for it to be present in our inner world, so that it is no longer pure imagination but comes to be a subtle reality.

Is holiness important in life? It might not be so in our secular society, where science did not interest itself in nor validate holiness, or where science had to oppose faith because of the political struggles between the Church and state, or where the word "holy" is now little used; all that does not exactly favor the corresponding experience. Perhaps it would be better if what was cultivated were a feeling that was already present in childhood, although it does not have a name, which has to do with wonder, with the sense of grandeur, with valuing of the other. For just as beauty is in the eye of the beholder, so is holiness, the holy, the sacred.

For the ancients, just as for the primitives, it seems that the sacred was not a problem: the earth was sacred, nature was sacred, the sky and the animals as well. The community itself was perceived as something sacred. Lévy-Bruhl spoke

at the beginning of the 20th century of the mystic participation of the primitive peoples, for whom the word "we"
was much more intimate than the word "I" and although at
first it would seem that they were confused about this word
"we." Now it would seem that instead the word "we" had
more weight for them, as they valued more the collective
participation than the separate activity or individual thought.

We say, then, that this evoking of the sacred is an important aspect of meditation. This is what the Christian precept
of "Love God above all other things" refers to, only it is not
necessary to have a theist vision or to use the word "God" to
sanctify life, people or things. It does not require a belief, or
a symbolic system, this love of the divine, which can also be
lived as the love of something called by various names, once
we understand it beyond the conceptual. Some people live it
as the love of life, others as the love of Dharma, love of the
intrinsic Buddhahood of conscious beings, others as a love of
the realization of their own potentials.

Finally, we all have an evolutionary thirst. We all feel a
metaphysical thirst, because we sense how we could be,
something like how a seed must surely sense the tree it
contains latent within itself. That aspiration to evolve, that
devotion to the path, that dedication to the inner work, to

the movement of consciousness, that is also devotion, which does not necessarily happen because of visualizing some bearded father or grandfather figure in the sky.

The Christian theologists of the first centuries knew this, those who formulated what is called Negative Theology, distinguishing that one thing is God (not visible to our eyes from here nor understandable through our concepts) and another is divinity, which we cannot conceive of with the conceptual mind. All religions have more or less the same experiences and equivalent forms of contemplation.

All the spiritual traditions say that devotion is a great journey and that the very aspiration already brings us closer to that which we aspire to. He in whom the flame of love of the divine burns has an advantage over others with regard to the necessary dissolution of the ego, moreover they come closer to the recognition that the divine is already present in their thirst for it.

If it is true that devotion is so important, is there not a way of introducing a devotional element into education, without reference to any specific religion? I think that this possibility is present in music. It seems to me that there is a lot of music in our classical European heritage that is intimately devotional. Bach, for example, signed his works adding the phrase *Soli Deo Gloria* to his name and therefore we can consider that the very act of composing was for him devotional and that in enjoying his music we participate to a certain degree in his devotion. Because the love of the divine is a gift from God to men, since the love of God is already divine, feeling devotion brings us closer to our nature.

But there are those who are ignorant of devotion and cannot imagine it, so that in order for them to come to know it they must search for and develop patience. Just as there are those who have absolutely no compassion (cold people, who cannot imagine how anyone else is feeling) there are those who do not know reverence or appreciate love and it would be good for them to become interested in opening themselves to that dimension of love that is the love that looks to the heavens, orienting themselves not so much to humans as to the ideal. Or toward something unknown that we would like to arrive at.

Compassion comes from the mother, being an extension of biological love, already developed by mammals, whose females recognize their children as another self, that is to say a 'you'. Martin Buber said that the ability to see a 'you' instead of seeing just 'things' is what would fix the world. I talk now though of admiration or appreciative love, which surely originally directed itself in our lives toward the father and was then was turned particularly toward the divine, the higher consciousness and ideals such as truth, beauty, goodness and justice.

My opinion is that the Great Music serves specifically for the exercising of this appreciative or devotional love that in a secular society disappointed by its ancient ideals has remained unexercised. We do not realize that music places us in contact with the sacred, since it has been over aestheticized and that tends to hide its spiritual relevance, so much so that we do not realize that the great musicians are mystics who use the language of music for something that it is not possible to express with words.

That is my view, at least: that the great musicians are the gurus of the Western World and they have fed us spiritually without our realizing it; showing us, among other things, how to feel higher emotions that are not those of our day to day experience. If we do not recognize the experience of the holiness in music, it is because it does not remind us of ecclesiastical music and because we associate holiness too much (it could be said) with the scent of incense. In a certain moment, ecclesiastical music separated from secular music and I think that the holiest music in that period (which coincided more or less with Beethoven) remained outside the Church. In this regard a famous woman of that time, named Bettina Brentano, explained in a letter to her friend Goethe that Beethoven should be considered the person closest to God of their generation.

To leave a strong imprint on human consciousness though, goes far beyond what we consider aesthetic and music is much more than an ornamental art of sounds, despite certain academics of music having adopted this overly narrow view.

Thus, just as the divinities are visualized in many spiritual traditions, whether these are African orishas, the angels and archangels of the Judeo-Christian world, or the Tibetan pantheon, I think that in an analogous fashion it is possible, through music alone, to reach comparable levels of enthusiasm. Let us not forget that the true enthusiasm is what lies in this word's own etymology: *en theos*, which meant an inspiration or possession by the divine. Listening to Beethoven's Ninth Symphony, we do not recognize the devotion it transmits to us through a relationship with the divine like that of Bach (which is a devotion that has many genuflections that corresponded to the attitude toward the divine in a time of monarchies). Paradoxically, this is due to the fact that in Beethoven's Ninth Symphony it is as if God himself spoke, so that listening to it is more comparable to the presentation of God in the text of Genesis.

If we wish to be transported by music to a higher world, we need to listen with an attitude that is a little different from the usual one. Normally, we listen with an ear that is somewhat consumerist, waiting for the music to come and give us something. Instead, we must approach the moment of listening to music as one in which we concentrate on generating a feeling of enthusiasm for the divine. Or more specifically, for the divine that we still do not know; that is to say, an enthusiasm for something larger than ourselves, which in aesthetics has been called the sublime. I think that this way of feeling originates during our forgotten early childhood in relation to our father. Just as little chicks follow the hen (according to that mechanism called imprinting that Lorenz was the first to investigate among ducks and which later has been understood as being universal), we humans, who receive nourishment from our mother, follow the model of the father, with whom a relationship of authority is established. Except that the origin of the authority lies in whoever gives it, no matter how much it has deteriorated over the course of history because of the thirst for power of the frustrated dominant males of our species.

In short, now as on so many other occasions, I take advantage of injecting into our secular, modern world something of consecration through the use of music and an invitation to make use of musical empathy, that is to say, to put ourselves in the place of the person who is singing, trying to identify with the sound and make our will be the will of the music. Music is expression and what I propose is to adopt the same expression that what we listen to transmits to us.

I still need to tackle another complementarity in the realm of meditation, whose apparently contradictory poles are love and detachment. About love, I will say that not just in the context of interpersonal relationships have practices been created to cultivate it but also in the area of solitary meditation; having already dealt with the development of love in a long earlier chapter, I will now refer only to detachment, which despite being the necessary antecedent to wisdom, barely has room in our culture.

We no longer have an ascetic culture and the tests of surrender of the spiritual cultures of the past seem suspicious to us, so that we interpret them as possible masochism or irrational superstition. Nevertheless, detachment might very well be the fundamental characteristic of the people we consider to be wise.

As I have said, someone who asks, "what is wisdom?" will at least understand that it does not consist of knowing many things but is a certain attitude toward life. If we take the next step in our inquiry wanting to clarify that attitude, we see that it is one that could be described approximately as looking at life from a certain distance, or with more perspective.

That distance that lets us detach ourselves from things, people, or experiences consists to a certain degree of our de-identifying with them, which has sometimes led to life being said to be like a dream.

This cultivation of detachment, or what we could also call the capacity for surrender, is another way of talking about what the Oracle of Apollo said (which we know about through one of the inscriptions of the ancient temple at Delphos): "Nothing in excess." Our lives are very excessive, because we have many false needs that appear to us as many desires, and our desires, intensified moreover to the level of passions, have even complicated our community life. Less attachment means fewer passions and less of all that which the ancients called the sins. The Fathers of the Church said that to find the love of the divine one had to develop apathy, a state of peace and neutrality that would be very easy to confuse with indifference for those who only know it from outside, trying to imagine it through words. *Creative indifference* was the term proposed by the German philosopher Friedlander (who we know primarily through Fritz Perls, the creator of Gestalt, although Harmut Geerkan will now publish in Germany the many volumes of his complete works) and I have sometimes used the expression *cosmic indifference*. It is said in Buddhism that compassion and wisdom are complementary paths that should be traveled in parallel and I think that the notion that compassion emerges spontaneously from detachment can be a relief for those who know how limited our ability to become more loving at will is, as Christian culture preaches we should do.

Our desires are problematic and without us fully realizing it, our desires are what separate us from our deepest nature. Therefore, there is nothing more liberating than the possibility of going beyond our desires, led by a deep spirit of surrender, which is like dying to ourselves.

One could think that the capacity for surrender is something that would be too large a subject for the education of youth, like approaching spiritual experience through contemplation, but let us not forget that asceticism has not just been a part of practically all religions but also part of the education of young shamans in cultures that in our arrogance we presume to have surpassed.

To conclude, some words about what the subtitle of this chapter proposes: "Education of the spirit beyond religions." Naturally, we need to come to an agreement about the meaning of the word "spiritual" and I would simply say that it does not seem to me that spirituality should be confused with religious beliefs or moral codes.

Obviously, thinking is not in itself spiritual, no matter how much time one spends thinking about spiritual subjects; nor do ordinary emotions like happiness or anger seem spiritual to me in themselves.

Although we cannot deny that the first historic religion was spiritual (tied to Dionysus in Europe and to Shiva in India), neither can we deny that it cultivated a form of spirituality (the surrender to spontaneity itself) not recognized as spiritual by Christianity.

To speak of a spirituality that goes beyond religious beliefs, we must look back to the reality of human maturity, whether this is transmitted through art or through the lives of the wise.

It is obvious that even though many think that it important for education to recover a spiritual relevance, advancement toward this has not been possible beyond a poorly formulated debate between alternatives like that of a Mohammedan or a secular education (or between an education whether Catholic or Protestant and the exclusion of religious subjects from school programs).

Depending on the country, there is a dilemma between the dominant religion of the territory or no religion at all, however now at the beginning of the third millennium, it is embarrassing that we have not transcended such a parochial situation to propose a universal religious education, such as is being done with regard to art. If in the field of artistic education one surveys all the styles and works of the most representative artists of all cultures, why are there no courses also being taught in western schools about the vision of life and the world as explained to us by the greatest religious geniuses of all cultures?

This would entail progress over and above our religious or secular parochialism, but we must recognize beforehand that it would not go beyond constructing a theoretical spiritual education and if we want to bring spirituality to education, that should not limit itself to theory or even just to words. It is in meditation where we find not just the possibility of a true spiritual education but also one that would not require dogmatism or ideologies. Even though the practice of meditation rests on certain points of view that can favor its practice, its introduction is possible in a way comparable to that of a good friend who says to another: "Hey, try this and you'll see for yourself what it offers you." The point of view that someone who meditates needs to adopt does not go beyond the construction of a provisory thinking that prepares them for the experience, without coming to comprise an ideology, to say nothing of an obligatory faith.

I said that there are many traditions and innumerable forms of meditation and that even within every traditional spiritual school there are diverse forms of meditation. Nonetheless certain universal characteristics of the meditative mind can be highlighted and if one, by optimizing the mind itself, becomes a better person, what is achieved is a multifaceted phenomenon impossible to describe with a single word. Therefore, because each form of meditation is also especially relevant for one or another facet of a complex phenomenon, it is worth describing what happens in the mind during meditation from a multidimensional point of view.

That is what I have already done through this exploration of the three bipolar dimensions that we can recognize in the area of meditative experience: the non-action and the permeability of the current of life; attention, which is the light of awareness and culminates in consciousness of consciousness itself and detachment; and love in its diverse forms, which include love of the sacred and compassion.

This set of inner states serves as an approximation to what has been meant by the similar but somewhat devalued term *spirit*.

CHAPTER 9

The SAT Program for the Development of Self-Awareness and Love

I. SELF-AWARENESS

SELF-AWARENESS IS THE HEART of psychotherapy, particularly the therapeutic trend that began with Freud and resulted in humanist psychology. Although it is not everything in psychotherapy (since the process of *liberation* of the true self is also important, the process of overcoming obsolete and conditioned responses of the past, as well as the surrender to the spontaneity of the current of life), self-awareness is a practically indispensable tool for such liberation. For only through the becoming aware of what happens to us can we leave it behind: it is through becoming aware of our limitations that we can overcome them; through becoming aware of our inhibitions and fears, we can try to move beyond them.

As certain as it is that self-awareness is what will let us leave aside our artificial forms of relating and our dysfunctional responses to love (acquired during the course of childhood, as answers to dysfunctional aspects of the personality of those who surrounded us), it requires a basic preliminary ability.

In a similar way to how an apprenticeship requires that we know how to listen and see, the awareness of ourselves requires that we can have access to our experience, in the moment in which such experience happens. Although it would seem that this awareness of ourselves were something intrinsic to our nature (just like the ability to see or to listen), it is not as certain that we are able to know what we feel. Instead, both on the level of our emotional awareness as on that of our bodily awareness, we perceive what happens in us much less than we know. There are things that we do not want to know that we are feeling and perhaps there are many things in our experience that we do not want to recognize, that we have hardened ourselves to a certain degree, becoming less sensitive than we could be. We have lost interiority, and as a reflection of this loss of interiority or awareness of the subtler aspect of our mind (our emotions, feelings, dreams, and thoughts) we have also lost something of the contact with the immediacy of our body; attention is just one thing, and if we absent ourselves from ourselves, that is reflected in more than one aspect of our attention.

Today, many schools of bodywork have emerged: the *new somatologies*, they have been called. Not just new forms have been discovered (such as the Feldenkrais method or Eutony) but people have also become more interested in ancient practices oriented toward awareness of the body and the subtle improvement of bodily function, practices that are related to the improvement of the most complex aspects of our psyche. The people who become interested in one of these disciplines, whether these are Reichian therapy or the Charlotte Selver school of bodily awareness, or so many eclectic forms of bodywork introduced by people who have learned from many sources, these people who embark on a path of bodily awareness soon realize how far they are from having an aware and harmonious body. We do not even ordinarily have a unified sense of our body. We can feel our face, our hands and our legs, as we guide our attention to them or move them but who feels their entire body as one? Probably, that is how it was when we were babies, when all our movements, moreover, were unified and implicitly coordinated. However, just as we have learned to think one thought at a time, following an analytic course of reasoning (and precisely, to the degree that we have learned to do this), we have lost the ability to see things in their totality and also in the corporeal sense, we have lost this feeling of a unified body. This could seem just a detail of little interest, an observation only made by those who dedicate themselves to becoming aware of their body (no doubt under the guidance of someone who already knows one of the corresponding disciplines) but no! Surely the unified awareness of the body has a lot to do with the awareness of being present, the awareness of existing, beyond the awareness of this or that.

The practice of attention is sometimes cultivated in immobility and then we usually refer to it as meditation. Nonetheless, the practice of attention is also present in every moment in the disciplines of movement, which are sometimes considered primarily as situations of attention to the body whereas others approach it with an emphasis on expressivity, which leads from movement to dance. All these situations, from immobility to expressive movement, imply a call to be there, therefore they are something like an antidote to a state of relative automatism in which we live, as if life were intrinsically painful and it suits us not to be too present in what happens to us.

It is in meditation when we focus our attention most sharply on our interiority. There are also degrees of inte-riority within it though, because sometimes we are more interested in knowing our emotional world, to be able to better understand what happens to us. Nevertheless on other occasions (or in the case of other meditation techniques) we are more interested in the heart of the inner world, which is beyond our emotions and also beyond thinking, in attention to simply presence, or if you wish, attention to simple existence, which is another way of talking about the continuity of attention in the present.

Today, the clinical and educational relevance of a form of meditation that is the basis of Buddhist practice is being discovered: the simple attention to the here and now, traditionally known as Vipassana, that has been making an entrance into the academic world, both of psychology as well as medicine, under the name of *mindfulness*. The bases of this practice are found in a Buddhist writing called The Four Foundations of Mindfulness, that is to say, the four fundamental elements of the practice of attention: the Satipatthana Sutta, which explains how bodily experiences, emotional experiences, the experiences of thinking and awareness of the mind itself should be systematically heeded; beyond thinking, feeling, or loving.

However the solitary practice of meditation has a disadvantage and it is that people can fool themselves and think that they are meditating, when in reality they are dreaming, or only imagining that they meditate. Therefore the martial arts are useful, in which bodily attention is cultivated not just with one's own movements themselves but also by paying attention to the movements of other people in one's visual field, in which distractions have an immediate response in the form of blows and a person who pays little attention soon ends up on the floor. In a similar way, the practice of attention can be enriched when transported to an interpersonal situation. To a certain degree this is what happens in various therapeutic situations but above all in the basic therapeutic situation of what is called Gestalt therapy. The basic exercise of this is one in which the patient narrates what they are perceiving moment by moment under the supervision of a therapist, who perceives their distractions, evasions and difficulties with remaining in the present, which manifest above all in the patient turning their attention toward the past, anticipations, explanations, or justifications.

When awareness of the living current of attention from moment to moment is practiced in a finely supervised situation, it is easy to discover that the process of recognizing what is happening in oneself involves a certain courage to be oneself and to communicate this in an authentic way. This courage, in turn, involves something like openness to the possible suffering of finding ourselves with unpleasant things, since ordinarily we feel rather important, having cultivated a good image of ourselves, not just for the external public but also for ourselves. However, when we explore our reality we realize that we are not as brilliant, special, important or perfect as we have been pretending to be to ourselves and others.

The process of exploring oneself is therefore something like a *descent into the underworld*, in which little by little we lower ourselves from our pedestals and perhaps dropping down even further, we discover what has been hidden under our pleasant everyday mask. This descent into the underworld does not just require an acceptance of suffering but also involves a growing need to accept ourselves just as we discover ourselves to be.

If simple attention to the present moment already involves the potential for this journey toward our hidden aspect and the interpersonal here and now, doing this in the presence of an expert leads us even more quickly along this journey, the addition of other therapeutic technique intensifies the process. In gestalt psychotherapy, for example, an experienced person can perceive the *polarities* in the life of someone who is doing one of these exercises and invite them to dramatize such apparently contradictory elements within them that must eventually be integrated. The companion, whether this is a therapist or a work partner in an exercise of mutual help, can also stimulate the person who is discovering him or herself to intensify the expression of the more difficult things to accept, in such a way that the process is thereby accelerated. In this way, a methodological repertoire arises (which is something like a development that must take place through the history of the psychotherapy) in the process of help.

Until now I have been talking practically about the awareness of what happens to us in the present moment. However, one thing is *mindfulness*, or the simple attention to our experience in the here and now, and another is actual psychological self-awareness, which encompasses things like realizing our own characteristics in human relationships, our personal style of doing things, which distinguishes us from others; everything that in the world of psychotherapy is called *insight*, which is not simply an intellectual understanding of ourselves, but an emotional or felt understanding.

The term originally arose in the world of psychoanalysis, where the understanding of *insight* has inspired the notion of what should be a good interpretation by the psychoanalyst in aiding the patient to attain self-understanding. Such interpretations seek not just an awareness of what happens in the present but also the relationship of this present moment with the past. More broadly, the understanding of ourselves is something like solving a puzzle in which the different pieces of understanding or partial observations of ourselves fit into a larger gestalt (whole), whose greatest expression is, perhaps, the understanding that a person manages to achieve of their life as a whole. Understanding our own personality plays a very important role in understanding our lives, since just as dramatists have always known that behind the fate is the character, all of us are understanding little by little that it is our attitude toward life (and more broadly our personality) that shapes our lives on a day-to-day basis.

Beyond these two forms of self-awareness (the self-awareness of the present moment and the extended self-awareness, that we could say embraces such things as the understanding of our human relationships, the root of our personal problems, our personality, and of our life itself, everything that could be summarized in the expressions "psychological self-awareness" or *insight*), there is a third form of self-awareness that is not psychological and is nonetheless a deepening of the process of becoming aware of the present.

We could call it "philosophical self-awareness," in that it is an answer to the old question of who we are. But the word "philosophical" has the defect of suggesting that it is a purely intellectual kind of understanding. An alternative would be to call it a "metaphysical self-awareness" but the word "metaphysical" also has its disadvantages, at an historical moment in which science has turned against the old philosophical discipline of metaphysics. In Buddhism this self-awareness is known by the technical term of *wisdom*, and its goal is described as the understanding of the mind's nature. Not just Buddhism has been interested in this deep understanding of ourselves though, which goes beyond the field of psychology or the movement of our emotions and behavior. Surely, when Apollo's Oracle gave Socrates that famous piece of advice: "Know yourself," it was not referring to a form of psychological understanding but instead to a question from that field of knowledge that the philosophers (or the wisdom traditions) have sometimes referred to as a deep reality: the raising of awareness to a reality beyond the obvious. Although some academic philosophers of today ignore the existence of such a deep truth, we cannot ignore that it is something that has interested the mystics of all times and which some have called God, the Tao, spirit, or Buddhahood.

With the framework of the above, I want to now explore the repertoire of techniques for the development of attention and self-awareness, in the framework of the SAT Program.

Vipassana

Vipassana is not just one thing but rather a bouquet of techniques. In my way of presenting it I have preferred to highlight this multiplicity instead of prescribing the monolithic practice of an identical exercise practiced over time. Having had the good fortune to find a series of masters of Vipassana, such as Dhiravamsa, Goenka, Rina Sircar from Burma, and others, and having felt that the diversity of formulae has been a help comparable to that of complementary points of view, which enable the essence of something not be confused with a specific vision, I have created an unusual program that brings together these variants of the basic practice of being in the here and now.

Here and Now

As a second component of this curriculum of attention to the present, I make another mention here of the basic exercise of gestalt, which its creator, Fritz Perls, called the *continuum of awareness* and which is commonly known as the *exercise of here and now*. This is one in which, in successive moments, the person translates into words their experience of the present, letting themselves be carried by a spontaneous preference in the choice with which attention passes from one thing to the next (given that the course of attention can follow very diverse labyrinths, passing from the sensorial to the awareness of movements themselves, to emotion, etc.)

Gestalt Exercises

Although the basic exercise of Gestalt is formulated in a very simple way, many variants on this can be created, in which a person accompanied by another works in a more specific way with what is emerging. For now, I will just say that an additional block of the SAT Program is made up of Gestalt exercises.

Free Association

A fourth resource is that of this method introduced by Freud that we could describe as a process of sharing what attention to our thinking reveals with minimal self-censorship. In my book *Between Meditation and Psychotherapy*, I have described some of the many variants of free association used in the SAT Program under the name of *exercises of shared observation of thought in a meditative context.*

Emotional Autobiography

I move now from the world of the exploration of the here and now to what one could say was its opposite pole: the panoramic vision that one forms of life itself.

Every person who enters our program is asked to provide an autobiography. Generally, when they reach the third year, I ask them to rewrite this autobiography, which reveals to a good degree how much awareness has been gained through the process of self-understanding, particularly since the program includes a detailed revision and the corresponding redrafting of the painful childhood experiences that person had with their parents.

It seems to me that life is an art that one practices in only a partially aware fashion, and that the more awareness one places on the processes of living, the easier it becomes for one to come to approach life itself. Many artificial lives are lived, and life is lived in a very passive way, being carried along by one's culture, one's family, one's friends etc.

People who begin to awaken from that process can become distraught, feeling that their condition worsens when confronting the challenge of freedom. Nonetheless, the process of transformation is like that: one in which this worsening is a stimulating factor to keep moving on.

People share a lot about their own lives during the course of the SAT process, in addition to having written an autobiography when entering the program. I would say that it happens more quickly than in ordinary therapeutic situations, in which people come to understand their lives from session to session. Naturally, a complete therapy is one that leads people to understand their lives better or more deeply. However I think that something is lost in not making this an explicit aspect of the therapeutic agenda and I like to emphasize that the very process of rewriting one's life story various times can be a kind of art that helps one to realize many things, that would happen much more slowly in the course of ordinary conversations, whether in the context of friendship or love. As these residential groups are an intimate community, people get to know one another more deeply, and part of the content of that mutual awareness is knowing about one another's lives, since people who are interested in the greater understanding of their own lives are naturally interested in sharing. People who share, begin to be interested in the effect that this transparency has with regard to what they have done with the life they have been given.

Psychology of the Enneatypes

Very briefly, I will mention now that, with respect to another aspect of self-awareness (that of awareness of personality) a set of notions and exercises that I have been calling the psychology of the Enneatypes (already explained in another chapter in this book) has been very important in our program.

The Hoffman Process

Another subject is the study and understanding of *the formation of the personality during childhood*, through the introjections and acts of rejection of the parental models, just as proposed by Bob Hoffman originally, in his individual work, today transformed into a group variant that has come to form a pillar of the SAT Program.

Mutual Therapies

Another significant opportunity for gaining self-awareness in the SAT Program, after the psychological exercises like the variations on free association and the Gestalt exercises, is a series of mutual therapies, which aim to stimulate improvisation, intuition and originality, in which attention is paid not so much to the techniques of psychotherapy as to the elucidation of the suffering (as in the analysis described in the first chapter). An important component of this work supervised by Gestalt specialists (who help each person to work on the difficulties they encounter when helping others) is, naturally, the ability of the apprentice therapists to understand and in turn contribute to the understanding of the person they are helping.

Review of the Transformation Process

Another aspect of self-awareness is the analytical reflection and the understanding of the very process of one's development, or the *process of transformation*: the analysis of the changes experienced since entering into the multifaceted group process that is our program. Just as the Enneagram offered us a map of the conditioned personality, we have an entire set of *maps about the journey*: explanations about the inner journey that have appeared in diverse wisdom traditions. Personally, I am interested in making a synthesis about what the transformation is and what is known about its stage, about its vehicles or various ways of working through which one can advance.

Another method or context is that of the most sophisticated or refined of the laboratories of self-awareness, which is the therapeutic context *ad libitus*. A therapy that differs from therapeutic exercises in that there are no rules, just a situation in which the individual works on their own perception and creativity in front of someone else, and in this situation an encounter factor comes into play, in other words the impact of one person on another.

Wisdom

Finally, there is wisdom. The metaphysical self-awareness, the search for self-awareness, for that seed of the soul that is stability, beyond the coming and going of thinking, feeling, and loving: *the search for the self* and the explanation of how the aspects of "peace" and "detachment" enter into it, along with explanations on the nature of the mind and the traditional explanations that help us to find it.

II. The Three Loves

Since the beginning of my work on the SAT Program, the inspiration of Tótila Albert about the unification of our brains and their functions has been present and also in what touches on an integration of the personal experiences of the father and the mother. However, it was many years later that, remembering a phrase of his ("being three who love each other") and evoking the image of the father, mother and child in a mutual embrace, it occurred to me that the embrace of our inner parts could be conceived of as an embrace between the three different ways of loving. Since then I have been thinking as well, that the different values of the three dimensions of loving underlie many of our conflicts.

If instead of simply associating our three brains with the instinctive, the affective, and the cognitive, we associate them with three different ways of loving, we can say that our reptilian brain is erotic, our middle or mammalian brain is rational and empathetic, whereas our neocortex, that which distinguishes us properly as humans, is associated not just with the intellect but also with appreciative love, that which is oriented toward the ideal.

The Christian precept already implies the notion of three different ways of loving by telling us to love our neighbors as ourselves and God above all things but to speak in this way does not make explicit that it is a question of different ways of loving in each of those three cases. Love of the divine or devotional love is of a different nature from maternal or charitable love that characterizes loving thy neighbor and on the other hand, the love we have towards ourselves is, in reality, something like a love of our inner child, with its desires and simple expectations of happiness.

The first task that I tackled after conceiving of this notion that our internal unification involves a balance of love, was to analyze the different personalities in the Enneagram from the point of view of these three nuances of affective life. It was easy to verify that effectively, each of them involves a particular imbalance. Thus, for example, fearful personalities are less erotic and more admiring; emotional personalities are more predominantly maternal; perfectionist personalities are predominantly admiring and repressive of instinct. The observation that each enneatype carries with it a tendency toward the underdevelopment of one of the loves that make our experience of life full was enough for this knowledge to be added to the psychology of enneatypes as a therapeutic recommendation.

How can the three loves be worked on? How can one who undertakes a path to self-awareness develop the kind of love that it best suits them to cultivate, in view of the chronic underdevelopment not seen until now.

A program based on this point of view could be conceived but in the case of the SAT Program I cannot say that this has been so in a conscious or explicit way. Rather, I have been giving form to this program to the degree that I have discovered the diverse resources that seemed to me relevant to a complete training. Only a posteriori, on explaining the map of the three loves, could I see that all of them were represented in diverse aspects of the program. I give a concise explanation below.

Pleasure-seeking Love

Or, *Eros*, which is still so problematic for many people even at the start of the third millennia, is gradually becoming decriminalized, we could say, thanks to the therapeutic activity since the times of Freud, who was the first to point out the mechanism of repression, the almost universal fear of castration and the antagonism between civilization and the pleasure principle. However, we could say that the effect of psychoanalysis on the liberation of people's desires was weak compared with the therapies that arose later, like Reichian and Gestalt. It is in Gestalt where it seems to me that the *spirit of freedom* reaches its culmination, as an implicit philosophy and as being the therapy itself, to the point that I have come to consider Fritz Perls as an apostle of Dionysus.

I begin, then, by mentioning Gestalt therapy as an anti-repressive theory beyond its specific techniques, in view of this implicit faith in the spontaneous impulses that I have called an *organismic faith*: the trust that our natural desires are good, no matter how much upbringing and education have shown us to mistrust them as if they were perversions.

Gestalt therapy is not so present in the SAT Program through the explicitly Gestalt workshops, which appear only in the third module and are given by experienced Gestalt therapists who work on the participant's problems when helping one another mutually. Nonetheless, Gestalt has been much more present in the Program than in just that explicit way. In the first place, because the population of those interested in the program when it took place in Spain for the first time, at the end of the 1980s, were precisely the people involved in this kind of training and this gave the successive classes a Gestalt culture beyond the specific activities in the program. Also, I have wanted the people who teach certain subjects, such as the psychology of enneatypes or spontaneous movement, to be people with a therapeutic ability and it is in the group of Gestalt professionals that I have found them, which has also contributed to the creation of a more permissive atmosphere than in other therapeutic groups.

I have said that there is already in psychoanalysis an element of helping people which is oriented toward enabling them to recognize their non-explicit and perhaps embarrassing desires and to end up respecting them more, integrating them into their lives in this way. The psychoanalysis in the SAT Program is presented primarily for its fundamental technique, which is the free association of ideas, in which a person lets their thoughts flow with minimum self-censorship and the sharing of these thoughts with the person who observes them. Maslow was correct when he wrote that the free association of ideas was something like a Taoist exercise of spontaneity and reading that observation was one of the elements that inspired my own experiments with this technique, already during my years of working in the Esalen Institute in the 1960s. Here then, is a second element in the SAT Program, in which people are invited to leave behind their tendency to control, at least in terms of knowing what they are going to say, daring to say things that they would not express in social life, due to being worried about the social consequences or their own image.

But a more specific and deeper method for letting oneself go, giving oneself to the spontaneous impulses of the moment with a minimum of calculation or inhibition, is the practice of Authentic Movement, which arose in the field of dance. Personally, I have transformed this discipline into something different that we call simply spontaneous movement, and which could be characterized as Authentic Movement without its Jungian rhetoric. Authentic Movement, just like spontaneous movement and also an exercise called *latihan* that has been cultivated in the Subud group, originally from Indonesia, is more than practices of movement, practices of surrender that does not just lead to motor expression but also to affective, imaginary or spiritual experiences and sometimes to phenomena of movement that do not seem to have their origin in life itself, such as experiences of possession or bodily energy fluxes. Although only a minority of people come to such experiences in our groups, they are particularly revealing and impressive, since they seem to involve an openness to a spiritual dimension of life, just like in the phenomenon of inspiration and more than anything else they resemble psychedelic experiences.

Psychedelic experiences are not part of the SAT Program (although in Brazil I have recommended the experiences of *Ayahuasca*, which are part of the local culture, to those who finish our program). However, the psychedelic world could be said to be the Dionysian world *par excellence*, given that in it, not only do the inhibitions that normally interfere with the deep spontaneity of the mind disappear with ease, giving rise to what is called the expansion of awareness but also from what we know, the Dionysian religion was associated in ancient times with the use of hallucinogens.

Thus, as the expression is associated among the ancients to the figure of Dionysus, more specifically, theater was a way of honoring Dionysus that the Greeks understood to be a sacred act. Theatre, when it is not simply the artistic representation of previously written works but is rather aimed at personal development, is yet another activity in which risk, improvisation and breaking free from inhibitions predominate, all of which at the same time benefit the development of the capacity for surrendering to spontaneity and creativity. This is so much the case that with the stimulus of an experienced instructor like those in our program, a person can go much further in their surrender than in the simple situation of spontaneous movement. This has been an important part of the SAT Program, which has developed in a creative way through my invitation of certain theatrical directors to integrate their professional experience with the learning of Gestalt therapy and their culture in the psychology of enneatypes. Their diverse contributions, in turn, have been integrated into what could be said to be a culture of *sui generis* therapeutic theater.

Compassion/Benevolence

I move now to compassion or empathy, and I will begin by observing that, quite often, in the course of effective psychotherapy, people do not just come to understand what they suffered during their childhood due to the insensitivity, violence, selfishness, and other psychological problems of the adults around them but they also transcend the chronic resentment they have lived with since then. In these cases, people have come to forgive their parents or other perpetrators of abuse.

What happens spontaneously and without a predetermined form through a usual therapeutic process, can be achieved in a more deliberate fashion, however, if one systematically searches for the person's episodes of suffering through their early life story and stimulates them to give full expression both to their suffering as well as to their rage.

I am convinced that everything that made us furious during our childhood and which has led us to break our early loving ties, become ambivalent or resentful or vengeful, can only come to be forgiven when we have first discharged the anger that when we were children it proved to be too forbidden for us to express or even to feel. Bob Hoffman was the person from whom I learned this therapeutic maneuver of leading people to vehemently express their rage, with the goal of later being able to leave it behind. I have already said something about this unusual person, who left us a method for the reestablishment of the broken loving ties with our parents, received through his mediumship and I have also dedicated a chapter to the relevant process, taken from my book *Change Education to Change the World*.

If one of the pillars of the Hoffman Process is the discharge of anger, in order to later be able to leave it behind, the other is *forgiveness of one's parents*, to later be able to forgive ourselves and the people who came later in our life stories. Although this echoes the Freudian vision that all our relationships with those who surround us bear the imprint of our relationships models learned in childhood toward our parents, only the Hoffman process seems to me to systematically apply this idea, making the essence of the therapy a healing of the original family relationships.

I consider that the contribution of this method by Hoffman, which was originally one that he applied in an individual way with his patients and which I later transformed into a group method of directed mutual help, is incalculable in view of what it adds to the scope of the old spiritual traditions that head toward the ideal of love. The fact that Christianity, despite being fundamentally a religion of love, has had such little success with regard to the intention of generating a less violent society than the one we have, is a demonstration of the fact that the path of love requires something more than good intentions and sermons. Primarily, the path of love requires that whoever undertake it crosses through the door of forgiveness. To take that step of forgiving someone involves leaving behind the mechanical conditioning of our personality, something that is sufficiently hard so as to require special help. In the case of this method created by Hoffman, this help consists of a process of understanding one's parents as a preliminary to being able to look at them with compassion. Also, in the context of this method, we are helped to understand that if we are not to blame for that which comes to us from our parents, they likewise are not to blame for a plague that came to them in turn through a contagion from their own parents. Various elements enter into play then, in a living process in which one person guides another to take that step of forgiving their father and mother; after which something changes in relationships, not just with one's parents but also with oneself and with other people.

I think that the Hoffman Process encapsulates an enormous potential for the world, both in the education of youth as well as in the training of teachers and of all those who help others in their own process of psycho spiritual development.

Perhaps the primary stimulus that participants of the SAT Program receive with regard to the development of compassion, aside from what has already been mentioned, is through their education in Tibetan Buddhism, in which the path to compassion is understood as one intimately associated with the development of detachment and the understanding of what is called the *no-self*, that is to say, the illusoriness of our ordinary image of ourselves, that serves as the nucleus of our selfish desires. It is as if, in the process of understanding of Buddhism, there were a step from personal identity to the identity of life itself, which helps us become less self-centered.

Appreciative/Admiring Love

With regard to appreciate love, I will begin by saying that something that has been very useful for many of those who are by nature disdainful (whether through their pride, their competitive envy, or due to problems with paternal authority) to understand the theoretical approach that a person who is not able to feel admiration loses something very important. It would seem that people who value themselves by devaluing others, would end up ahead; however, when one sees oneself as large and all the rest as tiny, life loses meaning. It is important to learn to bow down before that which is large, both in nature as well as with people, since in that appreciative gesture we fill ourselves with the value of what we can only perceive in this way.

This mere understanding, linked to the observation of demeaning tendencies and difficulty in admiring, make many narcissists begin to develop of the kind of love they are lacking.

Devotion

Traditional practice that is oriented toward the development of admiring love is what is known through the general term *devotion*. However, the traditional forms of devotion become problematic in our secular modern world. This is not just because they are seen to be intimately tied to a theist vision of the world which is no longer universal, or even the majority vision but because so many spiritual traditions converge in our cosmopolitan culture that their simultaneous presence in our awareness and environment, plays down their validity and apparent value. Even for those believes who hold the idea of a single God, through multiple manifestations, the situation of a visitor in Jerusalem could be difficult, where the father of the Holy Sepulcher competes with a muezzin proclaiming the oneness of God at the same time. We do not in fact, need to be in Jerusalem for something similar to take place.

It is here where we are helped by our comprehension that the multiple forms of devotion are alternative formulae of a same basic love: *appreciative love*, the range of which goes from respect to admiration, culminating in adoration.

Appreciative love does not just recognize values but also creates them, in a similar way to what is recognized in the saying that "beauty is in the eye of the beholder." What is important with regard to the sacred is the ability to sanctify and it is important that, when using the word God, we do not fall short by thinking that we know what we are naming. It would be better for us to think of the word God as a metaphor for something that we truly do not know and that only for convenience do we name it in some fashion, since otherwise, the concept of God would become a veil that blocks us from going beyond ourselves. But whether we say "God," "Buddhahood," "Tao," or simply "spirit," it is important not to fall into the idolatry of orienting our appreciative love toward a concept.

Appreciative love orients itself toward the ideal and encompasses values such as truth, goodness, beauty and justice. These are not mere concepts though, no matter how the secular world tries to reinterpret them in such a way, without being aware of what is lost when going from what the ancients referred to with the name of God to mere thinking.

It seems to me that one of the most important forms of devotion that the people who participated in our programs developed is the growing seriousness with which they work on themselves, because the motivation with which one works on oneself, in order to purify the mind of negative emotions and cultivate love, is equal to a call to realize one's own potentials, and the intuition we have of our potential is no different from our intuition of the divine.

What is more, the quality of the tie that is established between a seeker and their guide is something that becomes refined and deepened over time, in such a way that the transferential characteristics (belonging to the childhood ties) end up being left behind and devotion arises. Western culture has tended to question this devotion as a dependence or idealization, out of ignorance or from a mistrust of a kind of apparently antidemocratic authority, or from jealousy toward possible misuses of the same. Even though charlatanism and fraud exist in the world, there are in the living spiritual traditions ties of deep respect and of a devotion (associated with surrender) that is like some kind of fuel and a catalyst along the inner path. Where there is appreciation, one absorbs more quickly: it is as if there were a very direct relationship between devotion and grace, which is the reason for so much insistence on devotion as an opening to the possible blessing of the spiritual current that passes through the masters in history.

Music

Additionally, there is a resource for the development of appreciative love that is free of the need for beliefs and this is music, which probably arose in the world of the shamanic cultures as a form of elevation of awareness that has been broadly cultivated as a form of devotion in the western world and which continues existing in music beyond churches and beliefs.

Not only is music a vehicle of devotional love, or compassion, or Eros, as typically appears in romanticism but there are works that specifically stimulate appreciative love, with their sublime content or their mysterious profundity. When we talk of the classics, in music, we refer precisely to a certain artistic greatness that comes from the fact that the music becomes an implicit communication for us with a higher consciousness.

The great musicians of the Western tradition have been our spiritual guides, without us having been consciously aware of this. Once we do recognize the spiritual content of music, we can listen to it to even more avail.

I think that, in view of my own early musical training, teaching people to listen to music with ears that go beyond its beauty has been one of my most specific contributions, helping them to appreciate more subtle and specific values than even the word "sacred" seems to reflect, since we associate the sacred to such a great extent to acoustical atmospheres that remind us of ecclesiastical music of the past. So just as we must learn to recognize the divine beyond our childish or juvenile connotations of what God is, we need to discover the sacred beyond the limits of what smells of incense.

CHAPTER 10

The Rehumanization of Companies:

NECESSARY CHANGE FOR THE ECONOMY AND SOCIETY

SOME YEARS AGO, one of the instructors of a prestigious school of business administration asked me how a company could contribute to the wellbeing of its employees and I will begin this chapter with the answer I sent him as part of a letter:

Naturally, this seems an important subject to me, especially if it is understood in a broad sense, not limited to the working conditions within the walls of the office and during working hours. With regard to the latter, perhaps I am not the best person to comment, because I know little about the corporate environment and therefore I will limit myself to saying that perhaps the best thing that a company could offer its employees would be help with the care of their minds in the form of courses on personal growth.

I say this, in part, because the other things that occur to me seem impossible. Could a company perchance offer their employees the knowledge that what they are doing is a true service, for example? Personally, I think that it is important for our wellbeing to know that we are participants in a network of mutual services that is an intrinsic part of our social existence (just as Buddhism establishes, in its precept of *live correctly*, and implicitly all religions in their ethical precepts). I also think that it is not enough for the belief in the value of one's own work to rest on an instilled opinion through a propagandistic indoctrination, as is the case among many teachers, who consciously think that they are serving their pupils despite the fact that they unconsciously perceive the truth, which is that their activity serves above all to maintain the status quo and that which Eisenhower called the "military-industrial complex."

Obviously, it is impossible to fulfill this need that people have (as political animals) to feel socially useful in an intrinsically unjust and exploitative economic system such as the one that rules in the world today. That could only be hoped for in the event that the business world took part in a project of self-transformation that promised to turn it into a benevolent institution.

But is a project of humanizing the corporations conceivable as it goes against the grain of the far from benevolent nature of the macrosystem in which it exists? To what degree would it be possible for a corporation to offer its employees the chance to give a true service when its own statutes subordinate every goal to profit? In such a context, naturally, the word "service" comes to have a very limited meaning, although sanctioned by the everyday experience that everything we do to earn money serves the interests of some public.

In contrast with the dead end in which I see myself destined to end up while considering the question in its most specific sense, as soon as I consider the subject in a broader sense, I begin to imagine more interesting things to say; at least for myself and particularly in view of the special opportunity that sharing these with relevant people offers me.

Although I only start to consider it now, I suspect because I find the negative and symmetrical variant of the subject thought provoking, this is a good question: how the corporate world currently interferes with the human development of its personnel.

The answer to this seems very clear to me. Given the fact that corporations have been created to make money and that their statutes provide for the subordination of everything to profits, it is natural that both the executives as well as the employees develop a mentality that is congruent with such subordination of all values to money. This is the heart of the problematic issue, for in order to say it in the language of the ancients (which personally seems to me as clear and valid as it was for our ancestors, with barely any semantic adjustment): it is a sin to place money above God, or contrary to our wellbeing to place greed above the desire for psycho spiritual evolution (or the desire to serve a universal will).

It is clear that today, in the secular modern world, we are made to feel that the religious values of the past are something cultural and even more that they are musty or anachronistic. Do we not think that way today precisely because that is what best serves the corporate world? Is it not simply the case that no rival values are wanted in the empire of Mammon? The current dialogue does not even want there to be any weight given to the position of Mohammedan culture, which still prohibits speculative profit, that is to say, making money with money, without producing goods.

Even so, it would not be so easy for us to believe in the rhetoric of the ethical and ideological relativism that is in fashion if it were not because we never exactly understood what the ancients knew very well. Saint Thomas says that in every sin, one aspect refers to our behavior in the world and another refers to an implicit distancing from God. This, translated into the modern language of psychology, is the same as saying that there are pathologies or deviations of psychic energy that do not just have interpersonal consequences but also disconnect us from the depths of ourselves; they alienate us, they make us lose a healthy orientation toward the natural priority of the quality of our own consciousness.

Just as it was valid to say in another time that if we gave priority to the 'Kingdom of God', everything else would be "added unto" us, it seems valid to me today to say that if we do not give priority to the quality and evolution of our consciousness, everything else will prove to be (as we are seeing) a disaster.

Without trying to pretend that the top executives of big business are bad people and understanding that they do not do anything other than what they can within the rules of the game of our economic policy, I will open a space here to invite those of you who read this to value not just the disastrous way in which these rules of the game involve today a subordination of everything to merely economic considerations but also, the way in which this subordination corrupts us, dehumanizes us, makes us smaller and ends up causing uncountable suffering.

The expression *economic policy* is already revealing, because it reflects a conception of another time in which it was thought that the economy and politics should go hand in hand. Clearly, this is no longer the case, since politics (implicitly, the care of the common good, justice and morality) has come to serve the economy in the same way in which the large countries, industries and commercial or financial institutions have infiltrated or bribed parliaments and governments. Let us not forget that etymologically, economy derives from the Greek work *oikos*, "household" and that the implicit metaphor that assimilates the economy of a nation with that of a family takes for granted that, in both cases, the administration of the assets will adhere to the needs of the people and to considerations of justice (which will be spontaneous among people joined by loving ties). Just saying this reveals how the expression *economic policy* is a euphemism in our day. Just as the economy has dominated politics, it has also dominated practically everything else, asphyxiating life and its intrinsic values, the social order, and our institutions.

If we consider the most elemental of these, which is the family, it seems obvious for anyone that the growing slavery of parents to the market (to the degree that the world of the masses grows poorer and the middle class disappears) interferes not just with their individual quality of life but also with their ability to be mutually generous in their performance of maternity and paternity.

Also, it is a result of the lack of availability that parents have for their children that children are at the mercy of that institutionalized paternity that is the school system. And what is wrong with the school system? It serves this system of production and indoctrination in a conformity with the established order to such a degree that it now does not even recognize that it has ceased to educate. An ignorance reigns with regard to the difference between teaching and educating, to the extent that not even the unions and those who protest in the streets because of cutbacks in education know what to ask the authorities for other than salary raises and more of the same old things.

Needless to say, that what is said about education also applies to information beyond the schools. Far from having been a means of educating the community, as was foreseen in the years of the discovery of radio and television, it is obvious that the stupefying effect of the mass media on awareness, its use for the purposes of distraction, misinformation, conformity and manipulated democracy, far surpasses its educational effects. Just as Ivan Illich argued in favor of deschooling, Jerry Mander, in the US, has argued eloquently for the suppression of television. Why? Because the economic power has recruited the media to the service of politics that serve the economy and the politicians of the commercial nation (which has come to replace the nation state) and which is sold, like products, through its image, above all serving the interests of the companies, to which the majority of the stations belong.

It is obvious that all of this is nothing but the intensification of an even older unfavorable influence of the economy on human life which Marx already highlighted, just that personally I do not agree with his materialist interpretation of the priority of the means of production over everything else and I think that instead it had to do with something like a prioritization of illness over other things, despite its extreme seriousness. Thus, in the world there is both the passion for power of the exploiters as well as concern for the survival of the exploited, without any of these being of a properly material nature but obviously emotional and the result of a psychosocial dysfunction that is no less global than the economy.

In case this abstract affirmation might seem whimsical, let some specific images serve as counterbalance. For example, a lawyer in the times of Jane Austen could say that studying law had less to do with the spirit of justice than with the protection of property and however much their contemporaries might have disputed this, that is indeed the case for those of us who consider history, which shows us how in that same period the English opposed the Members of Parliament who proposed the cessation of their collaboration in the trafficking of slaves and how even in the Age of Enlightenment they resisted the idea of treating Africans as human beings.

To the degree to which, with the rule of neoliberalism, the rules of the marketplace (operating with the least interference to ethical considerations) are leading to a concentration of riches comparable to the old children's game of Monopoly (which is a good model of a pure economy), poverty has been feeding people's chronic obsession for survival that has been dragging the world to the often commented upon disappearance of values and the corresponding generalized corruption.

The ancients thought that education in virtue was a political priority, since only through people willing to do good can a happy society be conceived; but it was not from school that this moral education was expected to be learned, but instead from people's participation in the community and culture, and particularly from the laws. How far we are from being able to say in the modern world that the laws, habits and customs are educational, or that the legislators are the primary educators of the community! It is enough to think

that this is how things once were for the contrast to show us
to what degree our economy, supported by our legislation
and the governments of the civilized world, establish an education in selfishness and greed.

Said in other words: our unjust economic order educates
us as if it were designed to produce a kind of human being
like the ones conceived by the utilitarians and wrongly
attributed to Adam Smith: the *homo economicus*, moved primarily by his interests.[4] It is clear that not just the utilitarians
and the economists share that *gut* vision of the human being
but that this coincides with the Marxist conception and has
come to be shared by a large part of the general public, since
the economic reality of the collapses or those who feel in
danger of collapsing is not conducive to contemplation or
deep thought, nor are situations of stress compatible with an
aesthetic sense, or with the enjoyment of nature.

I will not go any further into these things that are half-
known and half-denied by the spirit of conformity in the
times in which everything can be questioned with impunity
except for the ideology of the marketplace, which has come
to take on the characteristics of a religious dogma not to

[4] It is interesting to see that this term so frequently used is a poor translation
of what Adam Smith used: self-love.

mention the audacity of continuing to attribute such ideology to democracy. I have only allowed myself to do this in order to give weight to my statement that as the "powerful gentleman Mr. Money" has increasingly taken control of the world, the more belittled human beings have become and society more dehumanized. Therefore, it is difficult to conceive of such a current project as that of the social responsibility of corporations without its leaders being fully aware of the damage that the exaggerated passion for profit that accompanied the development of the economic inequality in the first place and more recently, the development of modern super capitalism has done to society.

Just as in religious culture a process of conversion is recognized from which the formal adhesion to a church or creed is just an external sign when it is not a superficial substitute, it is also recognized that the essence of this process of reorientation of the psychic life lies in the understanding that until now one has lived in error. Modern psychotherapeutic culture also recognizes that in order to heal, people must first become aware of their illness.

No matter how much, for the masses of today, sin is an antiquated concept and illness is an anomaly of a few others, it is worth observing that just as sin is the condition of a fallen human race since mythical time immemorial for the Christian faith, also for Freud (and by extension for modern psychotherapeutic culture) illness is something that affects all of us to a certain degree through our participation in a society in which a universal neurosis prevails.

A neurotic person, according to this perspective, is nothing but a *normotic* personality who has become more aware and suffers to the degree to which they begin to understand the destructiveness of their incomplete, fragmented, and conflictive condition. Is it not clear that something similar would be necessary in order to change a human group?

It is clear that after taking advantage of the stimulus of the question about "What can the corporation do for its employees?" as an opportunity to contemplate the broader question: "How can the corporation serve the world?" My reflections have led me to affirm that corporations themselves must change, become humanized, take responsibility, etc. I think the first step toward that must necessarily be something similar to a group *metanoia*, if not of the entire business world, then at least of a group of pioneers with a philanthropic spirit who are interested in the project of placing such a process into effect.

I will not continue with the text of my letter but I will say that in my response to the invitation of the leadership professor I also presented my conviction that of all the good things that a united corporate front could do for the rehumanization of the world, none of them seemed to me to be as important and hopeful as helping toward the establishment of a true education, that would come to replace the one that we have invented, thinking more about production than human development or social health.

Even though many businessmen have already contributed to education and that will have surely benefited their good image, I doubt that they have contributed deeply to the good of the world, because it is of little benefit to the world to help the implicitly oppressive and secretly exploitative education that we have created. What would have been desirable for them to have supported and which corporate power could perfectly well make happen, is something very different: the transformation of education into an activity that more than helping students to pass tests or earn diplomas, works for wisdom and virtue, which are so outmoded in our corrupt world.

In view of the fact that my letter never received an answer and that has led me to doubt the sincerity of the rhetoric of social responsibility that inspired it, I feel moved to share my ideas with the community here, adding only briefly that since the rise of the financial crisis has become a burning question for the entire world, these ideas have taken on a new twist. My hope for a corporate initiative turned first on the hope for an inter-governmental agreement. Then I thought that, even though the subsidizing of the massive educational reform that could answer the multifaceted crisis of the western world should in all fairness fall to the business world in its totality, such an initiative should be taken into account by the World Trade Organization, or alternatively, through an agreement between nations, in whose joint power the possibility of creating a voice as powerful as that of the current transnational commercial agreements remains.

However, in view of the events of recent years, who could harbor such a hope in the political world of the modern commercial nations?

The transformation of education and even the transformation of the corporations themselves could only depend on the empowerment of the community outside of the institutions. And what should the future human community, already free from an evil domination, take into account in terms of directing itself toward the reform of its companies?

The Global Consciousness, Mass Criticism, and the Power of Delegitimization

I N HIS PROPHETIC BOOK, *Global Mind Change*, Willis Harman says that nothing produces quite as much change in a society as a change of consciousness in the community's majority groups:

> "The principal changes in societies over the course of history have not resulted from governmental decisions or from the outcomes of battles but from the fact that a large number of people changed their way of seeing things and sometimes only a little."[5]

Regarding the constitution of democratic governments in England and the US, he comments, foreseeing toward the end of the 20th Century, that we were approaching a historic moment like the fall of the Roman Empire, already corrupt despite its incomparable power:

[5] Global Mind Change. The Promise of the Last Years of the Twentieth Century. Knowledge Systems, Inc., 2nd edition, 1998.

"People must remember that no matter how powerful an economic, political, or even military institution is, this survives in view of its legitimization, which depends in turn on the perception of the people. People confer legitimacy or take it away, and the questioning of legitimacy is perhaps the most powerful force in history."

Through my own activism, I originally addressed the authorities, visiting ministers of education and sometimes even presidents of governments, trying to plant in their minds the seeds of a social transformation through a new education, but I have ended up dismayed by what could be hoped for from governments and their bureaucracies. As a consequence, I have become more and more interested in addressing the community itself, taking advantage of the opportunity of passing through different Latin American and European countries on my annual tour of workshops and imagining that if the politicians or the universities were to someday pay attention to the proposal that education must be thoroughly transformed to recover the relevance to human development that it always had for the best educators, such a thing would only occur as a response to the desires of the community.

Lately, even more disappointed, I think that perhaps we should not even wait for the community to influence the ignorant and perverse organizations that we have around us. As I have been saying since the beginning of this book, my most recent hope is that the community take charge of many things (or perhaps of everything) that it once delegated to its governments. It would be enough for us to have a unified worldwide community (or at least a unified Western community) to be able to begin to remodel our institutions, not simply in terms of education, commercial companies, or industries and administration but also regarding communications, finance, and so many other things, like maintaining peace.

It is my hope that someday intelligence, good will, and the power of a unified world community will come to be sufficient to free it from the ultra-powerful and shrewd systems in which our antiquated patriarchal civilizations in decline have culminated. I began this book wanting to contribute to the inevitable process of social transformation into which we are entering, taking place in the least-violent fashion possible, through the catalytic effect of a good understanding of our plagues and our potential health.

We have entered a new phase of transformation of the world since the advent of the financial crisis and especially since the beginning of the new form of social protest, unleashed by the now more obvious generalized irresponsibility of the financial-corporate government in whose hands lies the only power to which one can appeal.

With the intent of influencing politics by a call to heed the needs of the majorities that they have supposedly come to represent, the Indignados (the Outraged) who filled the Puerta del Sol in Madrid in May of 2011 were initially ignored by the Spanish government even though they stirred up numerous community protests in other parts of Europe and even against Wall Street, with the result that the sum of these public demonstrations have evidenced a considerable and growing social approval.

Edgar Morin has said that the Indignados lack an explicit statement of their proposals. However, it seems understandable to me that their insistence is that the most important aspect for now is to be heard in relation to their perception that the majorities should not continue to accept a supposed democracy in which "one percent governs by and for that one percent" and that politics can no longer serve only the interests of the corporations and money. A young woman among those who occupied the plaza in front of Wall Street said in response to this question:

"It makes no sense to make demands until you have power. If you make them too soon, you do not ask for enough, and you cannot insist on the implementation of what you are conceded. If they give you an election, for example, you cannot demand that the votes be counted well. We realized this soon in our discussions: we do not have the power to demand and that was difficult for many people to accept.

Instead of making demands, we formulate our principles, and the fundamental demand to put an end to corporate government, returning the power to the people. Once you establish that demand as your principle, you can choose any issue (energy, health, elections) and the solution becomes obvious. In the case of health, it is a question of removing insurance companies from between doctors and patients. In terms of finance, it is a question of fragmenting the large banks, so that there are not six banks who control seventy percent of the economy and transforming them into banks that serve the local communities, so that the money stays at home and does not go to Wall Street. In terms of energy, it would be to diversify the energy sources, so that people can have a source of energy on their rooftops, becoming producers of energy. We developed a saying: human needs before corporate greed. After that, everything was clear to us."[6]

The main difficulty, it seems to me, is for the Indignados to be understood by people like those who watched from behind the windows of their building on Wall Street, before which people had assembled to protest. It is one thing for their view to be understood by an average citizen, well informed and well intentioned, that the financial decisions of powerful speculators affected by the mania for enormous profits result in millions of poor people in the world who do not have enough to eat. It is quite another for them to be understood by the people specially educated in business schools and economic sciences, for whom human realities have been masked by the misleading language of economy, whose cold and neutral words allow for the hiding of massive crimes by making the death of millions appear to be the accidental result of principles as unalterable as the laws of nature.

Toward the end *Days of Destruction, Days of Revolt* by Chris Hedges and Joe Sacco (from which I took the above

[5] Chris Hedges and Joe Sacco. Days of Destruction, Days of Revolt. Nation Books, New York, 2012.

citation), they talk of a financial company whose stock index is the highest traded in the world and which buys up rice, corn, sugar, and livestock futures, raising prices up to 200% in the global market, in such a way that poor families can no longer permit themselves basic needs and literally come to die of hunger. Hundreds of millions of poor in Africa, Asia, the Middle East and Latin America do not have enough to eat because of this addiction to profit. The technical language learned in business schools and in the places where stock market transactions take place effectively mask the reality of what happens, which is mass murder.

The following sentence reminds us of the trial of Adolph Eichman, one of the perpetrators of the mass exterminations in the German concentration camps, whose crime, it was discovered, had been an exalted sense of bureaucratic duty and efficiency:

"The cold and neutral language of business and commerce is designed so that systems operate with a cruel efficiency, even though these are systems of death."

Toward the end of the book, pained by the abyss between the motivation that moves the bureaucrats of the financial world and that which moves him to indignant protest and

after an allusion to that vision of evil in totalitarian modernity proposed by Hannah Arendt (a blind, evil, banal, and
rootless, more than a radical evil sustained by demonic
beings), Chris Hedges writes:

> "In my lungs are the fibrous remains of the tuberculosis that
> I caught when, surrounded by hundreds of Sudanese dying
> of hunger, I worked as a foreign correspondent. I was
> strong, and my privileges let me heal, but they did not and
> their bodies, many of them of children, were thrown into
> mass graves dug previously. The scars I bear are whispers of
> those deaths, marks of those who never had the chance to
> come to be men or women, to fall in love or have their own
> children. I carried my scars to the gates of Goldman Sachs,
> and I threw myself at the feet of those merchants of finan-
> cial products to beg for justice because the dead and dying
> amongst the settlements and the refugee camps in different
> areas of the planet could not make the journey. They force
> me to remember, they force me to choose who I am with."[7]

Surely, the mere global awareness of the realities of our
political-economic aberration would be enough (just as
the deep understanding of the individual, neurotic mech-

[5] Ibid. p. 268

anisms would be enough) to begin to leave them behind but in what direction should we head as we begin to free ourselves from the great beast of the modern commercial patriarchy that has claimed the monopoly over terrorism?

A first ideological alternative that occurs to us is one somewhere between Gandhi's conviction that we must overcome the industrial development underlying capitalism and that of his contemporary Tagore.

On lucidly perceiving the pathological and dehumanizing nature of Western civilization, Gandhi proposed that India should reject the technological advances and defend its simple and traditional way of life. However, another Indian of his time (Rabindranath Tagore, who, on the other hand, was the first to give Gandhi the name Mahatma) was of another opinion and thought that India should incorporate the valuable fruits of progress. Now that our tecnology has led us more than ever to that "decline of the West" described wisely by Spengler at the start of the 20th century, the question as to which of them was right remains a valid one.

I imagine that it was Tagore, according to an analogy taken from the process of the development of the individual mind. Because we are born into a sick world, we become sick developing a *neurosis* that we could conceive of as a parasitic existence that originally served us to defend ourselves from the environment that surrounded us during our infancy. We could refer to this part of the mind that has served us as a protective shell as our ego or personality, but the words are not very important. What is important to understand is that the process of a healthy human development is not merely a physical growth and learning, but also a process of understanding one's limiting personality, which makes it possible (through a healthy and liberating self-awareness) for one to free oneself from its interference with subsequent maturity. Those who come to achieve it know that the abilities that developed originally as part of their neurosis are not lost but instead remain at the disposal of the liberated adult mind.

In a similar way, I think that not just the industrial development but even much of commercial and corporate life could benefit our future, although not serving an unbridled lust for profit but rather servicing the community.

As I am no specialist in this matter, I will not venture to imagine how that transformation could be from our current technology in the service of patriarchal power to a technology in the service of the common good, or from a corporate world that services profit making to a socially responsible corporate world, or from an economic life in the service of the rich to a just economic life. To do so, it would be enough for us to leave aside the modern (antisocialist and ultraliberal) prejudice against the regulating function of governments and we would find ourselves with the solution to the current corruption or the excesses of economic power.

I also think that we should be careful of excessively planning things that should take shape through an evolutionary process and an extended dialogue over time, as free as possible from ideological dogmatism. Primarily, it is my belief that, in this as in other things, it is better for us to concern ourselves with our minds as a guarantee of the good results of our actions. If we hope for the humanization of our current corporations, nothing would be more relevant than the personal development of the people working in them. If we want to one day achieve political health, having politicians who are above all free and whole human beings, emotionally healthy and caring is more important than ideologies. More broadly, there is nothing from which we can we expect so much with regard to the transformation of our patriarchal institutions as the transformations of the people who comprise them.

As the inventor of a method of extraordinary efficiency and unprecedented speed, it is natural that I hope for the application of the SAT Program to the training of corporate administrators and public servants as it has already been applied to the training of therapists or educators. I also think that its application to these new contexts will require creative adjustments and by saying that I can have faith that I have created an efficient methodology for personal development, I do not mean that my way of working in groups is the only possible way.

Recently, Jerry Mander published a new book about capitalism[8] that bears a subtitle, the precision of which, seems to me, to embody the clarity of the opinion that is already becoming that of the majority since the financial crisis and of the successful persuasion campaign of the new peaceful civil disobedience movement: "Fatal Flaws of an Obsolete System." After devoting the penultimate chapter to the subject and question of "capitalism or happiness," he ends up in the twelfth and final chapter, with what is perhaps the most sensible reflection that I have read about alternatives for the future. I liked the fact that, like the Indignados, it is not based on authority, nor does he speak as a fanatic of any of the existing ideologies. He recommends that, like the Chinese, we remain open not just to dialogue but also to

[8] Jerry Mander: The Capitalism Papers: Fatal Flaws of an Obsolete System. Counterpoint Press, Berkeley, 2012.

experimentation with different economic models, and the most promising of the alternatives he lists seems to me to be cooperativism, in which the owners of the companies are the workers themselves, as in the Mondragon Cooperative Corporation in Spain. More important than the design of an alternative world, surely, would be the design of a process of transition from the current economic dictatorship of the global empire to self-government of the world community, and this is precisely what Ross Jackson writes about in his book *Occupy World Street: A Global Roadmap for Radical Economic and Political Reform*, in which he proposes a strategy that will bring together in a planetary league (*the Gaian League*) a limited number of nations along with innumerable civil organizations and representatives of the international community, to form the initial nucleus of an alternative system with its own alternative organization of commerce, banking, court of justice, and other institutions.

Without ignoring that the health transformation of the world that is now evidently necessary for our collective survival should involve a new economic practice and even a new economic science, which does not try to make the realm of commercial transactions a closed system removed from the environment and human needs, I am inclined to think that what is most important is not so much a new theory but a return of power to the community and a return of priority to the environment and fairness. Above all there must be a return to that which the title of this chapter proclaims: The Global Consciousness, by which I mean something more than ways of thinking or even of acting.

When Willis Harman wrote the aforementioned book, the most important thing for him in the change of consciousness that took place in the second half of the 20th century was the move from materialism to idealism. It seemed to him, in view of this, that "a new Copernican revolution" was taking place in the 1960s. It seems to me though that such an analysis still remained on the intellectual or theoretical level and that the greater consciousness of the public of today, which allows it to distinguish truths that were inaccessible to it until recently, is something that should be formulated beyond the area of beliefs, no matter how such beliefs tend to accompany the awakening of that higher consciousness that we have always associated with the religious, the esoteric, and certain kinds of philosophy. What Harman contemplated about this was, beyond a new idealism understood as a philosophical faith, the awakening of people's intuitive consciousness, particularly after the collective influence of hallucinogens in the 1960s. Only if an ideological change came from the evolution of actual awareness, would we have reason to rejoice. But Harman was not wrong in thinking that such a change was taking place and it also seems to me that a true increase in the level of global consciousness has been revealed lately, one already finds children who are more aware than those from other generations, as with the fact that people are becoming so receptive to a perception of how ridiculous and pathological the patriarchal ego is (both systemically and individually), with its narcissistic egocentrism, its unconscious castrations, its devouring shallowness, and its alienation.

By proposing then, that our hope lies in global consciousness, I refer to something more than the ideas of youthful revolutionaries or their preference for new requirements and standards. Without doubt, much will depend on the depth and quality of sacrifice of the caring spirit, but no less important will be consciousness as such, in the sense that the term has when thinking of more or less aware people, one speaks of "the paths of consciousness" or one says that the New Era consisted of a "revolution of consciousness;" a sense that implies *levels* in human development that entail a growing wisdom and ability to raise oneself above one's own smallness.

It is especially interesting that the degradation of politics in our time may have coincided with a silent progress of consciousness (or of awakening, or of being) in a considerable fraction of the population. Level of awareness has a contagious aspect to it and when the number of those who are awakening reaches a certain critical mass we can expect that phenomenon that has been described as *the effect of the 100th monkey*, in allusion to the observation, decades before, of what is said to have happened on a certain Pacific island, will begin to operate. It seems that the monkeys who lived there rejected the tubers that the humans offered them until one female decided to wash them in sea water. It was a stroke of luck that a group of scientists could be present to describe how, a certain point having been reached, some began to imitate the others who had discovered how to do it. Until this moment, they had merely observed the birth of a new cultural element: a phenomenon of collective learning through which the monkeys of this island came to be characterized by the new behavior of washing their potatoes. The unexpected part is that some informers state that when the number of monkeys who washed their potatoes reached a certain critical mass, the monkeys of neighboring islands also began to wash their potatoes, as if their discovery no longer needed to be transmitted through observation and imitation.[9]

This phenomenon, as well as comparable observations on the influence of learning through means which until now have remained unknown (such as, for example, the greater dexterity of mice in navigating labyrinths, as if the experience of other mice in other laboratories had influenced them), led the biologist Rupert Sheldrake to formulate his theory of *morphogenetic fields*. But we do not need to understand morphogenetic fields to harbor the hope that global consciousness, when reaching a certain critical mass, will have a contagious effect; different from the effect of mere persuasion, that will illuminate even those who, until now, have remained obstinate to removing the blindfolds from their eyes.

Our consciousness is pure lucidity, beyond the things that this lets us understand, just as a mirror is beyond the things

---

[8] The controversy regarding the scientific validity of the effect of the 100th monkey remains even today. In general, skeptics generally state that the original investigation of the Japan Monkey Center on the island of Koshima in 1952 does not prove that the washing of tubers spread to other islands save through the action of a washing monkey who swam to the next island, or instead they brand the whole episode as an exaggeration. Science or myth, this story applies very well to the current expansion of interest in awareness.

that it reflects, its virtue of reflecting reality depends on its receptive emptiness and its detached neutrality. Therefore, it is important that we interest ourselves more in our lucidity, which requires dispassionate neutrality, than in beliefs. But the formulation of consciousness as pure Apollonian spirit whose healing power rests in knowing how to see from a distance would be incomplete. We also need an ability to become transparent to life in a Dionysian surrender.

I used to say that the essence of that New Era that stimulated a generation of seekers in the 1960s, infusing a greater awareness into the therapeutic sphere and into the social movements, consisted of a new shamanism, not just in light of the great interest in the shamans of other cultures, but because it seemed that the Shamanic search was being rediscovered. This is a search for health that nourishes itself on the recognition of the illness and an aspiration to becoming complete beings, the impulse of which is the recognition of our fragmentation and incompleteness. I said that the most defining aspect of shamanism is not so much the figure of the artist healer, the mystic who is also interested in the empiric knowledge of nature, or in the role of the priest and guide, but the vocation of discovering depth itself, just like faith in the path of surrender to an organismic or animal intelligence.

Today, however, I would say that it is more precise to describe shamanism as a conjunction of the Dionysian path of surrender to natural impulses with the apparently opposite (but in reality complementary) path that the Greeks associated with the god Apollo, who cures plagues, is associated with the inspiration of the oracles and self-awareness but more essentially represents detachment, which shamanism cultivates through tests of painful austerity.

Dionysus, as the representation of the wisdom of losing oneself in passion, and Apollo, as the representation of the wisdom of dispassionate neutrality, presided over different mysteries in ancient times and the eventual reinstatement of such institutions are sorely needed, since they would make us better, both for the depth of the neutral consciousness that is the antidote to our small passions, as well as for the freedom of the Dionysian spirit, in which Nietzsche already saw the counterbalance to our repressive culture.

In saying that we must cultivate our consciousness then, it is important to conceive such a task both in its paternal and transcendent aspect, its Apollonian aspect, as well as in its inherent maternal aspect. Forgetting this complementarity makes us too cold or too bestial, when in truth it is not a question of the one or the other but of one of those mysteries that cannot be explained in words: a coincidence of opposites that entails the disappearance of our small, limiting daily self and a recovery of our intrinsic freedom.

I am now coming to the end of this chapter with which, in turn, I conclude my book. Asking myself what has remained unsaid, it seems pertinent to me to reiterate the political vision of Tótila Albert, poet and prophet still barely known, who for me was like a spiritual father and who was the first to denounce the patriarchal order, in the Germany of the interwar period. He then proposed that our species has not just crossed through a patriarchal phase in which the government has proceeded in a hierarchical or pyramidal structure, but also through an earlier matristic form of tribal or communal government, apparently established with the start of sedentary life in the Neolithic period. Before this we went through a filiarchal or anarchical phase of prehistory in which the governance of everyone by themselves predominated. He insisted on thinking of these three possibilities of social imbalance as transitory but necessary solutions to historic circumstances and he stated that we have not yet come to live what he called *the equilibrium of the three*–at which we could one day arrive through having the determination to no longer serve the patriarchal order.

There is a frequently cited phrase from the Book of Proverbs, of the Old Testament, that "when there is no vision, the people perish" and in our present ruled by the modern spirit of deconstruction and a suspicion of all the great theories, the vision of an alternative to the dying patriarchy of our time seems important to me as not just a vaguely democratic order, or one that is merely matristic, equally divided or fair, but more precisely one that is *integrative* of the three aspects (paternal, maternal and filial) that comprise our nature.

Since Tótila Albert lived in Germany in the years of his illumination, he called that healthy world that he conceived of as a possible future for humanity *Dreimal Unser*–an expression that would literally translate as 'three times ours' or 'the world of the three', in implicit reference to the Our Father of our patriarchal time that only recognizes the divinity of the heavens, while it tramples Mother Earth and sacrifices the Son. Naturally, in a triune society of self-realized people, the recognition of the divine would be as Father-Mother-Son. What would such a society be like, in which the maternal and filial values were no less appreciated than the paternal values?

Aside from the disappearance of the oppression towards women as well as of the castrating authoritarianism over the desires of children, the imperialism of reason as well as the denigration of the body and of pleasure, it seems to me that this Message of the Three would be psychologically expressed as a balance between the three loves, and politically as a heterarchical order among the three forms of government that we have known over the course of history.

Obviously, our world is still far from love, with the systematic lack of compassion of its politics and its economy and with its implicit criminalization of pleasure through upbringing and what is called "education." Even admiring love, formerly expressed through religiosity and patriotism, consisted in general of a falsification of a true devotion, sustained by conformity. Now that this has become manifest, our collective lack of genuine enthusiasm with respect to the true values is also revealed.

If we are to come to a society richer in love, we must pass through the encouragement of individual human development, on which I have already dwelt in the chapters dedicated to the reform of education, and I only need to add that it would be very desirable that the future courses for the experiential training of teachers also include the parents of the students, together with the teaching staff of the schools.

But, how should this political regime that I have called heterarchical be imagined, to distinguish it from the problematic hierarchical patriarchal regime?

We have already wanted to approach a synthesis between central government and government by the community in the Republican model, in which one expects a balance between the executive branch and parliament but obviously, we are far from what would be a true synthesis between democracy (in the literal sense of government by the people for the people) and monarchy (in the original sense according to which the king-priest embodied or interpreted divine will). Surely, it would not be possible to implement such an idea upon the basis of an election of representatives by the community, also for a direct democracy to be possible, government must be regional and not national. If we wished to opt for a model of government in which the rule of wise kings, specially educated in wisdom and virtue, as Plato conceived, were balanced by the communist or communal principle through dialogue with the regional community, it is obvious that this would only take into account the paternal and maternal aspects of that trifocal government. The filial aspect would be represented by the power of each citizen over their own life, that is to say, by a healthy element of anarchy that established limits to the prerogatives over the individual both of the central government as well as of the community.

I cannot stop feeling that two aspects of this political vision deserve to be kept very much in mind during the period of deep social transformation that is approaching. The anarchical aspect, which is in danger of being neglected when the communal enthusiasm threatens to become group tyranny, and the hierarchical aspect, which is in danger of being devalued because of an antiauthoritarian excess (understandable when we come from ridding ourselves of a corrupt and discredited patriarchal order). As someone who knew Carl Rogers and his enthusiasm for the self-organizational power of groups, I understand those who want to be wary of all authority and feel it unnecessary but I also think that the community itself will understand the value of the principle of authority, that we should not discard but simply contextualize in such a way that the hierarchical principle be inserted into a heterarchy alongside democratic and anarchic principles.

Although the new era that was already glimpsed in the 1960s, with its neo shamanic and Dionysian spirit, was interrupted by the counterrevolution of the threatened patriarchal system, the spirit of seeking as well as the perception of the need for a counterculture have been going through a slow and silent gestation and it seems to me that what emerges now is the maturation of that lucid and free consciousness.

If it has been the transformation of individual consciousness through a greater psychological understanding (Apollonian) and a greater personal freedom (Dionysian) which now finds a collective voice against the old and always refined evil collective, threatening to turn its back on it, this serves as a stimulus for us to have the faith and hope that we only need to continue growing and that everything else will follow.

I fervently hope that we try to be supportive when life gets rough and that we do not lose the joy while we attend to the rescue operations during these times in which our ship is sinking.

I have sometimes compared our imminent leap toward the unknown with the Exodus out of Egypt and its enslaving regime in the legends of the Jewish peoples. The comparison has seemed opportune to me given that crossing the Red Sea was followed by traversing a desert, which is offered to us as a good analogy of the situation in which we will possibly find ourselves that will require us to adapt to the scarcity of a less favorable environment. The image of a people following their portable altar with the Ark of the Covenant also lends itself as a suggestion that our success will depend on a strong orientation toward higher intuitions. More recently, it occurs to me that our situation also resembles that of the return of the Jewish peoples to their land after being exiled in Babylonia; since although freedom from the empire of commercial patriarchy will be like remembering a forgotten existence during years of alienation and finding ourselves free to reconstruct a world in accordance with our true values, our situation will also be that of constructing in the midst of rubble and confusion. Therefore as I say that during the times when our ship is sinking we must pay attention to preparing the lifeboats, I appreciate that my master (Tarthang Tulku Rinpoche) devotes himself to the preservation of the Tibetan spiritual legacy through the publication of thousands of texts for the spiritual training of his companions in exile. It seems to me that these treasures of wisdom are a precious heritage of humanity, no less than the Amazon forests, that we shall some day appreciate as a vital resource for our collective evolution.

I explained in my book *The Agony of the Patriarchal Order* that, in a meeting of the American Association of Humanist Psychology held in Toronto, I heard Willis Harman say that during the metamorphosis of a butterfly, in the chrysalis not only do the old structures disintegrate but a new central construction emerges built from cells that through their function of control over the development of the future organism, (as if they were provided with their design) have been called *imaginal cells*. It seems to me that the seekers of that time, for their dedication to their own future, will be the imaginal cells of the future world. It also seems to me that the seekers of today and of tomorrow will become experts in the process of transformation not just because of a vocation for self-realization but also because of a particular instinct for the wisdom of the masters and the immemorial traditions, through which they shall become essential mediators. Just as Moses and the other prophets in the roots of our spiritual culture were above all people able to hear the subtle *voice of heaven*, it would be a shame that in our understandable disillusion with religious and political authorities and in our egalitarian democratic zeal, we lost the ability to learn from the wise.

Claudio Naranjo was born on November 24, 1932 in Valparaíso, Chile. He was initially trained as a classical pianist, but quit the National Conservatoire when he began his medical school studies in Santiago–graduating in 1959.

A curiosity for further psychological and spiritual knowledge ultimately led him to the Esalen Institute in California, where he became the apprentice, and later successor, of Fritz Perls–the father of Gestalt therapy.

The death of Naranjo's son in 1970 prompted his return to Chile, a time he says, "marked the true beginning of a contemplative life and feeling of inner guidance."

Thus began his spiritual pilgrimage at the Arica Institute under the guidance of spiritual teacher, Oscar Ichazo. Together, Naranjo and Ichazo introduced The Enneagram into the Western consciousness, interweaving the teachings with modern psychology.

At the end of 1970, Naranjo left Arica after six months, and began coordinating with his mother, former Gestalt trainees, and friends, to bring the Seekers After Truth Program to life.

The 'SAT' Program consists of Gestalt therapy, the Enneagram of Personality teachings, meditation, music, and theatre as therapeutic resources. The program has been operating for nearly twenty-five years and has been an unmatched source of spiritual and psychological growth, healing, education, and change for many seekers, therapists, educators, and many others.

Dr. Claudio Naranjo passed away on July 12, 2019, at the age of 86, at his home in Berkeley, California. His legacy remains as one of the greatest Chilean thinkers, devoted educators, and pioneers in integrating transpersonal psychotherapy and the spiritual traditions.

The Revolution We Expected

OTHER TITLES FROM SYNERGETIC PRESS

RECLAIMING THE COMMONS
*Biodiversity, Indigenous Knowledge,
and the Rights of Mother Earth*
By Vandana Shiva
Foreword by Ronnie Cummins

SECRET DRUGS OF BUDDHISM
*Psychedelic Sacraments and
the Origins of the Vajrayāna*
By Mike Crowley
Foreword by Ann Shulgin

THE ANTHROPOCENE
*The Human Era and How it
Shapes Our Planet*
By Christian Schwägerl
Foreword by Paul J. Crutzen